THE JAINA THEORY OF PERCEPTION

THE JAINA THEORY OF PERCEPTION

PUSHPA BOTHRA

MOTILAL BANARSIDASS
Delhi :: Patna :: Varanasi

Indological Publishers & Booksellers
Head Office : BUNGALOW ROAD, JAWAHAR NAGAR, DELHI-7
Branches : 1. CHOWK, VARANASI-1 (U. P.)
2. ASHOK RAJPATH, PATNA-4 (BIHAR)

ISBN 0 8426 0874 5

First Edition : Delhi, 1976

Printed in India
BY SHANTILAL JAIN, AT SHRI JAINENDRA PRESS, A-45, PHASE-1, INDUSTRIAL AREA, NARAIṆA, NEW DELHI-28 AND PUBLISHED BY SUNDARLAL JAIN FOR MOTILAL BANARSIDASS, BUNGALOW ROAD, JAWAHAR NAGAR, DELHI-7

FOREWORD

I have great pleasure in writing a foreword to a work which was written during the years Mrs. Pushpa Bothra and I were engaged in studying together some of the original sources of Jaina philosophy. In fact, it was largely her interest which led me to study the Jaina logical and pro-logical works, and I found that for an understanding of the various problems and issues which dominate Indian epistemological discussions nothing is more helpful than the Jaina philosophical works. Partly owing to their ethics of non-injury, the Jaina Philosophers never rejected an opponent's point of view without conceding its element of truth; the resulting theory of *naya* led to the development of one of the most comprehensive meta-philosophical theories in existence. They thus prove to be honest, patient and careful expositors of the points of view of the other schools, but they also excel as thorough and systematic critics. It is only to the disadvantage of writers of other schools of Indian philosophy that they do not betray that thorough knowledge of and systematic reflection on the Jaina doctrines which the Jainas show with regard to theirs. Compared to the Jainas' comprehensiveness and scope, the others appear provincial and dogmatic. From an exclusive concern with the Nyāya and Vedānta, it is refreshing therefore to turn to Jaina philosophical writings: there is a breath of fresh air, an aura of tolerance and a spirit of consideration for the other's point of view.

However, not all is satisfactory with their own theories. But which school in the long and hallowed tradition of philosophy can claim to have all well about itself?

If epistemology (*pramāṇa śāstra*) is the basis of Indian Philosophical thinking, theory of perception (*pratyakṣa*) forms the basis of epistemology. For of all ways of knowing, perception certainly is the most primary. It is primary not merely in the sense that inference, our other main way of knowing, depends upon it and presupposes it, but also because our very sense of reality is derived from perceptual experience—so much so that philosophers who believe in a supersensible reality also believe in some mode of knowledge of such reality which is sensible but perceptual. To say that something is *real* is to say that it *can* be encountered in perceptual experience, though the reverse may not hold good.

Indian philosophers who have concerned themselves with ancient Indian epistemologies have been rather too much preoccupied with their theories of inference. Theories of perception and theories of linguistic meaning have suffered from comparative neglect: yet it is these which are philosophically more instructive. We have reason therefore to be grateful to Mrs. Bothra to have brought out this work on the Jaina theory of perception.

I want to draw attention to a few singular features of this theory. First, with regard to the concept of *pramāṇa* in general, the Jainas by refusing to count any non-epistemic factor as a *pramāṇa* and by requiring that a *pramāṇa* must be of the nature of knowledge are in effect maintaining that the phenomenon of knowledge is *sui generis* and cannot be accounted for by non-epistemic causes. This is what seems to me to be the strictly philosophical truth in the thesis that knowledge is of the essence of the individual self, that it is not acquired, that what seem to be the causes of knowledge are really instrumental in removing those hindrances which obscure the full manifestation of it. In the next place, with regard to perception, the Jainas begin with a rather strict definition of what should count as perception and required that perceptual knowledge should be not only immediate but should not be caused by the senses—which, in other words, is the same as saying that true perception is such immediate knowledge as does not require the mediation of the senses. But on this definition only the perception of the mystics, the *Kevalajñāna*, or at most the supposed perception through clairvoyance or telepathy, deserve to be called 'perception'. However, the more down-to-earth thinkers of the later period were willing to relax the requirement, and distinguished between ordinary, empirical perception and extraordinary, non-sensuous perception. In any case, the common mark of perception is that it is *viśada*, and this property of *vaiśadya* is further explained as clarity or *spaṣṭatā*—which gives rise to the question if vague, unclear perception is not perception or whether unclarity is a property of the object (as Sartre would like to say).

I would also like to emphasize the novel conception of sense organ, according to which each sense organ has two aspects : a physical and a psychical. Other important elements of the Jaina theory of perception are : denial of indeterminate (*nirvikalpa*) perception; denial of the thesis that the sense-organs have to reach the respective objects and be in contact with them in order that appropriate perceptual cognition smay arise; refutation of the Buddhist thesis that the object of perception is nothing but a form (*ākāra*) or content of that knowledge and not an external object; and of course the multifarious manner in which the Jaina metaphysical thesis that every real is both substantial and changing and in fact has infinite aspects comes to bear upon theory of knowledge.

Mrs. Pushpa Bothra has done a good job in presenting a lucid and highly readable exposition of the cardinal points and main arguments of the Jaina theory of perception.

J. N. MOHANTY
Professor of Philosophy,
University of Oklahoma.

PREFACE

In this book I have tried to give an exposition of the Jaina Theory of Perception, with special reference to the logical writings of the Jainas as distinguished from the Āgamika Literature. The Jaina logicians like Akalaṅka, Prabhā Candra Vādideva and Hemcandra have dealt with the nature of perception in great details and have extensively criticised the theories of perception of the Buddhists, Naiyāyikas and the Sāṁkhyas. Though much is known about the theories of perception of the Buddhists and the Naiyāyikas, adequate attention has not been paid to their criticism by the Jainas. In this respect Dr. Nagin J. Shah's book *Akalaṅka's Criticism of Dharmakīrti's Philosophy* (published by L.D. Institute of Indology, Ahmedabad, 1967) is the most welcome addition to the literature on Indian philosophy. Of the several books on Jaina psychology, recently published, mention may be made of the works of Dr. M.L. Mehta and Dr. T.G. Kalghatgi (Jaina Psychology, and Some Problems on Jaina Psychology respectively). These books are no doubt valuable contributions to the study of Jainism. They discuss to some extent the Jaina Theory of Perception, but their interest has been mainly psychology and not epistemology. I have however approached the problem chiefly from the point of view of epistemology.

I have not gone into the details of the Jaina Metaphysics except for problems which directly concern the Theory of Perception. I would frankly confess that my knowledge of the other systems of Indian philosophy is rather limited. However, I have tried to make use of some source books for these systems. Also I would like to mention that I have avoided any comparison with the Western Theories of perception.

This work was carried out under the supervision of Dr. J. N. Mohanty, Professor of Philosophy, University of Burdwan and was approved for the award of D. Phil. by the University of Calcutta. I am grateful to Dr. Mohanty for his able guidance and valuable suggestions. Many of the Jaina texts I studied under the late Hirakumariji, to whom I owe a deep debt of gratitude. I am also grateful to Dr. Hari Satya Bhattacharya, the profound Jaina Scholar for his valuable suggestions. I should also express my sincere thanks to Lala Sunderlal Jain, proprietor, Messrs Motilal Banarsidass for taking keen interest in the publication of this book.

PUSHPA BOTHRA

ABBREVIATIONS

AGT	*Akalaṅkagranthatrayī*
AS	*Aṣṭasāhasrī*
JBP	*Jñāna-Bindu-Prakaraṇa*
NAV	*Nyāyāvatāra-Vārttika-Vṛtti*
NB	*Nyāya-Bhāṣya*
NKC	*Nyāya-Kumuda-Candra*
NM	*Nyāya-Mañjarī*
NVV	*Nyāya-Viniścaya-Vivaraṇa*
PM	*Pramāṇamīmāṁsā*
PNT	*Pramāṇanayatattvāloka*
PVT	*Pramāṇavārttika-Ṭīkā*
PKM	*Prameya-Kamala-Mārtaṇḍa*
SS	*Sarvārtha-Siddhi*
SK	*Sāṁkhya-Kārikā*
SD	*Śāstradīdapikā*
SR	*Syādvāda-Ratnākara*
TB	*Tattvārtha-Bhāṣya*
TSV	*Tattvārtha-Ślokavārttika*
TS	*Tattvārtha-Sūtra*
TV	*Tattvārtha-Vārttika*

CONTENTS

PART : TWO

EMPIRICAL PERCEPTION

PART : THREE

NON-SENSUOUS PERCEPTION

PART : ONE

KNOWLEDGE AND PERCEPTION

CHAPTER I

NATURE OF KNOWLEDGE

1. *The relation between Self and Knowledge*

Knowledge is defined by the Jainas as *Svaparabhāsī*. The nature of knowledge is to be self-revealing as well as object-revealing. In other words, knowledge reveals both itself and the object. If knowledge were not itself known, it could not make its object known. The nature of knowledge may be compared with a lamp. A lamp reveals its object only while revealing itself. Knowledge, like a lamp, both reveals an object and reveals itself.

The Jainas hold that the relation between the self and its knowledge is one of *bhedābheda*. In one aspect knowledge is non-different from the self, and in another aspect knowledge is different from the self. Knowledge is the essential quality of the self. In this aspect, knowledge and self are identical. The Jainas reject the *Naiyāyika* view of complete difference between knowledge and the self.[1] According to the *Naiyāyikas*, knowledge is an accidental quality of the self, and there is a complete difference (*bheda*) between the self and its knowledge. Knowledge is an attribute which inheres in the self substance which, however, is separable from it. The Jainas point out that if the self and knowledge were totally different then there would be some relation between them. The relation between them cannot be conjunction or *saṁyoga*, because this relation is possible only between two substances, not between a substance and its quality. Further, the more relation of *Saṁyoga* between two different things, cannot cause a perception of non-difference between them. If the relation between them is taken to be *samavāya*, then also there would be difficulties. If there is a difference between the thing and the *samavāya* relation, then one may ask, what is the relation which relates the thing and the *samavāya*? If the thing and its quality are related by *samavāya* and the *samavāya*

1 *ŚR*, I, p. 51.

is related by another *samavāya*, then there would be an infinite regress. Therefore, *samavāya* relation is not possible between the self and its knowledge. Thus in this aspect, knowledge and the self are identical and non-different (*abheda*) in the same way as fire and its heat are non-different.

The *Advaita Vedāntists* hold that knowledge is the very stuff of the self. There is no difference between the self and knowledge. The self is knowledge as such. Śaṁkara rejects the distinction between substance and attribute; there is, according to him, no perception of difference between a substance and its qualities. A quality is an intransitive property of a thing and hence cannot have a reference beyond the thing itself. Substance and its quality are identical in the same way as fire and its heat are identical. Thus there is no difference between the self and knowledge.

The Jainas, who believe in the doctrine of *anekāntavāda*, do not accept either complete non-difference or complete difference between the self and knowledge. They assert the relation between them is one of *bhedābheda*. They point out that although knowledge is the essential quality of the self and there is non-difference between the two, sometimes in practice (*Vyavahāra*) knowledge and self may be called different, when the self is used as *kartā* and knowledge is used as its *karaṇa*; just as heat is the essential quality of fire. But sometimes 'fire' and 'hotness' are used in such a way that they are taken to be different (*bheda*) as when one says, "Fire burns by its hotness", where fire is *kartā* and hotness is *Karaṇa*, and the two are different. In the same way self and knowledge may be different in practical use (*Vyavahāra*), as for example, when one says, "One knows by knowledge" (*Jñānena jānāti*). Thus in one aspect there is non-difference between knowledge and the self, and in another aspect they are different. The Jainas do not accept the *Nyāya* view of complete difference and the *Advaita* view of complete non-difference between them. They hold that they are neither completely different nor completely non-different. Difference and non-differences are based on different aspects.

2. *Is knowledge eternal or non-eternal?*

The Jainas accept knowledge as both eternal and non-eternal but in two different aspects. In one sense, knowledge is eternal, and in another it is non-eternal. Knowledge is eternal in the sense that it is the essential quality of the self. There is no self without knowledge whether an object is present or not. Even in the state of liberation, the self possesses knowledge. Thus in one aspect, that is when knowledge is regarded as the essential quality of the self, it is eternal. But in another aspect, that is to say, in the sense of empirical knowledge, knowledge is non-eternal. Empirical knowledge is perishable. It arises when its object is present, and it disappears when the object is absent.

3. *Sākāra Jñānavāda and its Criticism*

According to the Buddhists, knowledge possesses the form of the object, because knowledge arises from the object. The Jainas reject this view. They point out, that knowledge cannot be of the form of the object, because knowledge is immaterial and what is immaterial cannot possess the form of what is material. The sky, e.g., is immaterial, and cannot have the form of material things. What possesses the form of an object is material, just as a mirror. The mirror can possess the form of the object because it is itself material; but knowledge cannot take the form of the object because it is immaterial. Everybody would agree to the truth of immateriality of knowledge. If knowledge contained the form or image of the object, its image would be imperceptible, because knowledge being very subtle is imperceptible. What is material is perceived only through the senses; it cannot be perceived without them.

That knowledge possesses the form of the object is not proved by perception; rather it contradicts perception, because everybody experiences his own knowledge of an object, as 'I know the jar', while nobody experiences a knowledge as containing reflection of the object in a mirror.[1] If knowledge has the form of the object then there would be no experience of difference of time and space of the objects; the object would not be experienced as being far or near, past or present. It cannot also be said that the judgments of distance, etc., are due to the real distance of the objects which cause the knowledge, for we do

1. *pratyakṣavirodhāc ca ; pratyakṣeṇa viṣayākārarahitam eva jñānaṁ pratipuruṣam ahamikayā ghaṭādigrāhakam anubhūyate na punar darpaṇādivat pratibimbākrāntam. PKM.*, p. 103.

not experience the distance or pastness in the mirror. If knowledge possesses the form (blueness) of the object, it should also possess the materiality (*jaḍatā*) of the object, as much as its blueness. If knowledge possesses materiality then it would be material, and if it does not possess the materiality then how is the materiality apprehended? If materiality is not apprehended, then the blueness also would not be apprehended. Otherwise either the two would be different or identical; if they (the blueness and the materiality) are different, then how can it be that the apprehension of the one (blueness) is also the apprehension of the other (materiality)? If it would be so, that is, the apprehension of the one may be that of the other, then the apprehension of one pillar may be also the apprehension of the whole universe.[1] If with the blue the material also be apprehended, then are they apprehended in their own two different forms? If it be said that the materiality is apprehended by a knowledge which does not have the form of that materiality, then why should not the same be true of the blue?[2]

The Buddhists argue that if all knowledge were formless, then there would be no difference between knowledges of different objects and every knowledge would know all objects. The Jainas, however, point out that this is not true, because every knowledge has some limitations and powers (*yogyatā*) due to which it apprehends only one particular object, it does not apprehend other objects.[3] A lamp does not have the form of the jar which it manifests and yet it manifests only this object and not all objects, owing to certain limitations.

Further, if the knowledge had the form of the object, then the knowledge would become a *prameya*, it would not be *pramāṇa*, because the object is *prameya*. A knowledge cannot be both *pramāṇa* and *prameya*, because they are two different things; *pramāṇa* is internal and *prameya* is external, so they are apprehended in different ways. The sense organs do not apprehend the form of sense knowledge. Knowledge is apprehended as knowledge of the object, not as the form of the object. Knowledge is always of the form, "I know", while the object is manifested

1. *grahītasya stambhasya grahītaṁ trailokya* rūpaṁ *bhavet. PKM*, p. 104.
2. *tarhi nīlatāpy atad ākāreṇaivānena pratīyatām. Ibid.*
3. *pratiniyatasāmarthyena. Ibid.*, p. 105.

without reference to the 'I'. Therefore the two cannot be identical. If the object were a form of the knowledge, then one would feel "I am the jar", which is absurd.[1]

4. *Is knowledge Svaprakāśa or paraprakāśa?*

The next important question is, how is the knowledge itself known? According to the Jainas, the Buddhist *Vijñānavādins*, the *Prābhākaras* and the *Advaita Vedāntists* knowledge is known by itself. Knowledge is by nature self-revealing, in the sense that it does not require anything else to reveal it or to know it. According to this view, knowledge is never an object of knowledge, but it immediately reveals itself.

Though all these schools of philosophy agree as to the self-revealing character of knowledge, yet there are some differences amongst them with regard to the precise nature of knowledge. According to the Jainas, knowledge is both self-revealing and object-revealing. The *Vijñānavādins* agree that knowledge is self-revealing, but they do not accept the existence of external objects apart from knowledge. They believe in identity of knowledge and object so that knowledge cannot be said to be revealing an object. The *Prābhākaras* are nearer to the Jainas than the *Vijñānavādins*. For, like the Jainas they believe in the existence of external objects. According to the *Advaita Vedāntists*, knowledge is the essence of self or Brahman. As such, knowledge is self-revealing or self-shining. On the other hand, some like the *Nyāya-Vaiśeṣikas* and Kumārila hold knowledge as not self-revealing. According to the *Nyāya-Vaiśeṣikas*, knowledge is known not by itself but by another knowledge known as *anuvyavasāya*. Kumārila holds that knowledge is not self-revealing because it is by nature non-perceptible, and is to be known by means of an inference, known as *jñātatāliṅgakānumāna*.

Hemacandra agrees[2] that knowledge is self-revealing or *svayamprakāśa*. In the judgement "I know the jar", like the subject and the object, the knowledge also is manifested. If the knowledge were not itself known, it could not make its object known. If we require another knowledge to know a knowledge, there would be the fallacy of infinite regress. Further,

1. *PKM*, p. 106.
2. *PM*, p. 3.

if it be said that the knowledge is known only after the object is known, there would be the fallacy of circularity, for the object cannot be known unless the knowledge is known. It cannot be objected that if knowledge is known then it becomes like another object and so ceases to be knowledge. For, when knowledge is known it is known as knowledge, just as the subject is known as subject and the object is known as object. In fact, there is no fault if knowledge becomes an object of knowledge, for it is knowledge in relation to its object, and it is an object in relation to itself.[1]

That knowledge is self-revealing may be proved by the following inference: Knowledge reveals its object only while revealing itself, for it reveals, as in the case of a lamp. A lamp both reveals an object and reveals itself. So also is knowledge. We may also infer as follows : Whatever is not self-revealing does not reveal an object, as in the case of a jar.

Thus the Jainas define knowledge as *svaparavyavasāyijñānam*. Knowledge is that which reveals itself as well as the object.

There is no person who knows the object without knowing that he knows it. To know an object means one must have the knowledge that he knows it. Thus knowledge of an object is known automatically with the object. For example, when one sees the jar in day time, he sees the light of the sun automatically with the object. In the same way, when one knows the jar he automatically knows that he knows the jar.

(a) *The Vijñānavādins' View*

According to the *Vijñānavādins*, there are no objects apart from cognition: a particular piece of cognition is possessed of a particular form. In other words, if objects exist, they become objects of knowledge through ideas which take the form of objects. Therefore, we are conscious of ideas and things together, the two are, therefore, not different. There is no difference between object and its knowledge. There is no difference between blue and knowledge of blue. All the properties are subjective forms. There are no objects independent of us; when we speak of such, we use words only. Outer objects are

1. *arthāpekṣayānubhūtitvāt svāpekṣayā'nubhāvyatvāt. PM.*, p. 3.

non-existent. These are fictitious. Due to some defect in eyes one sees double moon; in the same way, the objects seem to us as real but there is no existence of outer object, apart from knowledge. The object and its knowledge are one.

This is rejected by the Jainas. They believe in the existence of objects, apart from their knowledge. Knowledge is self-revealing as well as object-revealing. The Jainas ask: How is it known that cognitions alone are there? Is it by perception, or by inference? They point out that it cannot be known by perception, because the knowledge that there are only cognitions would require the knowledge that there are no objects. But the non-existence of objects cannot be apprehended by perception, because without an existent object perception is not possible.[1] The Jainas reject also the view that outer objects are fictitious like the double moon; one may perceive owing to defective eyes; the right knowledge of one moon proves the existence of the moon. If perception cannot prove the non-existence of object, inference also cannot prove it. For, all such inference will be contradicted by perception; and so will become invalid.

The *Vijñānavādins* may argue that the law of *sahopalambha* proves that the object and its knowledge are not different but one. The Jainas do not accept this; they point out that an object and its knowledge are not non-different, for, there is no perceptual knowledge of their non-difference.

Knowledge and object are not one, only if they are apprehended in the one and the same time. In the day time, the colour of an object and the light of the sun are apprehended together but they are different.[2] In the same way, the fact that knowledge and object are always together apprehended cannot make them one.

Again, the Jainas ask, what is meant by the word *Sahopalambha* used as the *hetu*? Does *sahopalambha* mean the simultaneous apprehension (*yugapad*) of the object and its knowledge? Does it mean the *more absence of apprehending them one after another* (*kramenopalambhābhāvaḥ*)? Does it mean that only one thing is apprehended (*ekopālambha*)? In the first case, if *sahopalambha*

1. *na tāvat pratyakṣaṁ bahirārthasaṁsparśarahitam. PKM*, p. 77.
2. *rūpālokayoḥ bhinnayor api sahopalambhaniyamasambhavāt. Ibid.*, p. 80.

means simultaneous apprehension of object and knowledge, then the *hetu* would be *viruddha*, because, the word *saha* is used in order to relate two different entities as, "The teacher comes with (*saha*) the disciple." The *saha* does not make them (knowledge and object) one. And if there is a difference between the two then how can they be called identical? In the second case, if *sahopalambha* means 'mere absence of apprehending the object and knowledge one after another' (*kramenopalambhābhāvaḥ*), then the *hetu* would be *asiddha*, because both the Vijñānavādins and the Jainas reject only such non-existence. If *sahopalambha* means the apprehension of one, because there is no difference between object and knowledge, then what is meant by the 'one'? Does 'one' mean the identity of the two, the object and its knowledge? If *sahopalambha* is used in the sense of identity of knowledge and object, then the *hetu* would be *Sādhyasama*. Since knowledge is internal and object is external entity, how would their identity be perceived? Again, when you say that 'one' is apprehended (*ekopalambha*) then is it meant by 'one' only knowledge or only the object? If 'one's apprehension denotes only knowledge then the argument would be fallacious because there is no difference between object and knowledge, according to the Vijñānavādins. If the Vijñānavādins mean by "one apprehension" only that of the object then how would the object be apprehended without the existence of knowledge?

Thus, the Jainas reject the *sahopalambhaniyama*.[1] They hold that object and its knowledge are not one but they are different. An object can exist apart from knowledge. There is difference in their nature. Knowledge is of the nature of apprehender (*grāhaka*), and the object is of the nature of the apprehended (*grāhya*). If there would be no difference in their nature, then the object could apprehend knowledge.

The *Vijñānavādins* ask, if knowledge is different from the object and it manifests the outer objects, then how does it manifest the outer object? In order to manifest the object, does knowledge have some activity or not (*savyāpāra or nirvyāpāra*)? Does knowledge possess some form or not (*sākāra or nirākāra*)? Does knowledge manifest its object in one and the same timeor in different times? In the first case, the Jainas would reply that

1. *grāhakasvarūpaṁ hi vijñānaṁ nīlādikaṁ tu grāhyasvarūpam. PKM*, p. 88.

knowledge apprehends the object by its very nature of manifestation. Knowledge is of the nature of manifestation and the object is of the nature of manifestedness. Therefore the objection that if knowledge knows itself, it cannot also know the object, is not valid.

In the second case, knowledge is neither *nirvyāpāra* nor *savyāpāra*; it manifests itself and the object due to its very nature, just as the lamp manifests itself and the object without requiring to be *active* in some other way. There is no need for any *Vyāpāra* for manifesting the object.

To the third alternative the Jainas would reply that knowledge is formless.

In the fourth case, the Jainas point out that those who believe in momentariness of objects, cannot ask the question, whether knowledge manifests its object in one and the same time or in different times, because for them knowledge and object both are momentary. The Jainas further point out that knowledge may manifest the object in different times also, as in the case of inference. Thus, with the help of above arguments, the Jainas prove that the object exists, apart from their knowledge; and knowledge is self-revealing as well as object-revealing.

(*b*) *The Nyāya-Vaiśeṣika View*

The *Nyāya-Vaiśeṣikas* believe in the theory of *paraprakāśa*. According to them, knowledge is not a knowledge about itself, for its whole nature is to apprehend its object and not itself. Thus knowledge cannot be known by itself. Knowledge itself is known by a mental perception. Just as an object is manifested by a knowledge, so one knowledge is manifested by another. First, there is the *knowledge of an object* (*vyavasāya*), and then another knowledge of that knowledge, i.e., there is an after-cognition. The *Nyāya-Vaiśeṣikas* call it *anuvyavasāya* of the first knowledge.

According to the Jainas knowledge reveals both itself and its object. In the judgment, "I know the jar", one not only knows the jar but also that he knows the jar. In other words, if the knowledge were not itself known, it could not make its object known. The nature of knowledge is comparable to a lamp; just as a lamp manifests the object and itself, and does not require another light to manifest itself, so also knowledge does not need another knowledge to manifest itself. If knowledge is known by another knowledge, then that other knowledge must have some other knowledge to know it, and in this way there would be an infinite regress.

The Jainas ask, what do the *Naiyāyikas* mean by *knowledge of the object* ?[1] Do they mean the manifestation of *only* the object, or the manifestation *also* of the object (along with other things) ? The Jainas point out that in the first case, i.e., if they mean by the manifestation of the object, the manifestation only of the object, then there would be the fallacy of *pratyakṣa viruddha*. Because, there is not only the perceptual knowledge of the object, everybody knows that he knows the object. If one knows the blue he cannot know the blue without knowing that he knows the blue. An object is apprehended by the manifestation of its knowledge, therefore there is no difference between the manifestation of an object and that of its knowledge. An object is manifested by knowledge, therefore the manifestation of the object proves the manifestation of knowledge. For example, when one apprehends blue he also apprehends its nature blueness; in the same way, when knowledge manifests the object it manifests itself also, i.e., when one knows the object, he also knows that he knows the object; without knowing that he knows the object, he cannot know the object.

In the second case, i.e., if they mean by manifestation, the manifestation also of the object, then the Jainas would agree with them for they also accept the manifestation of knowledge and also of object. Thus in both cases, whatever they may mean by knowledge of object, the manifestedness of knowledge is also proved.

According to the *Naiyāyikas*, knowledge is known by another knowledge, the first knowledge is known by a second knowledge. And it is because the two knowledges happen in quick succession that we do not notice their difference.

The Jainas reject this view. They point out that the same account should lead one to accept the doctrine of momentariness

1. *kiṁ ca arthagrahaṇaṁ buddhi ity atra kiṁ arthasyaiva grahaṇaṁ buddhī ity avadhāryate, kiṁ vā arthasyāpi ? NKC*. p. 184.

of every thing. For, one could argue that owing to quick succession the moments are not distinguished.[1]

Again, the Jainas ask : at the time of second knowledge, is the first knowledge present or not? If the first knowledge is present at the time of the second knowledge, then the *Naiyāyikas'* own thesis will be contradicted, because, according to the *Naiyāyikas*, two or more knowledges cannot co-exist at the same time. And if the first knowledge does not exist at his time of second knowledge then there would not be any process of knowledge. Because the first knowledge would disappear when the second knowledge will appear; the sense knowledge would disappear when mental perception will appear. How could the mental perception of the first knowledge take place when the first knowledge itself does not exist?

Again, the *Naiyāyikas* argue that knowledge is not self-revealing. It reveals only its object, not itself. If knowledge reveals itself by its own nature then there would be the fallacy of *pratyakṣabādhita*, for knowledge itself is known by mental perception. It cannot be known by itself as a sword cannot cut itself. The objection that if knowledge knows itself there would be the difficulty that it would be the object of its own activity (*svātmani kriyāvirodha*) is also not valid, for the *Naiyāyikas* accept that God's knowledge is self-revealing and it is universally well known that a lamp manifests itself. If there is no contradiction here, there cannot be any contradiction in taking all knowledge as self-revealing.[2]

The next argument of the Jainas is that knowledge does not produce itself but it manifests itself, just as a lamp does not produce itself but manifests itself. The *Naiyāyikas* point out that just as an object does not manifest itself knowledge also cannot manifest itself. The Jainas reply that this is not true. They ask : what do you mean by saying that a knowledge does not manifest itself? Do you mean that knowledge is not apprehended in outer space in the same way as an object is apprehended? Or, do you mean that just as knowledge is directed towards its object, so it is not directed towards itself? In the first

1. katham evam sarvabhāvānām kṣaṇikatvaṁ na syāt, *NKC*, p. 186.

2. *īśvarajñānena pradīpādy ālokena ca anekāntāt, na hi īśvarajñānaṁ svaprakāśane jñānāntaram apekṣate. Ibid.*, p. 187.

case the Jainas would agree with the *Naiyāyikas*, because the external objects like jar etc. are apprehended in space, but knowledge is an internal object, and so cannot be apprehended in outer space. If knowledge is regarded as imperceptible on the ground that it is not perceived, like outer objects in space, then the Jainas could also say that outer objects are imperceptible on the ground that they are not perceived, like knowledge, within.

In the second case, i.e., if the *Naiyāyikas* mean that as the knowledge apprehends the object, it cannot apprehend itself, then the Jainas would reply that this is not correct. For, the judgment, "I know the jar", shows that the object, the jar, and its knowledge, both are known. If it be doubted whether the latter is known, there may also be doubt whether the former is known.

Again, the Naiyāyikas ask, what do the Jainas mean by saying that knowledge manifests its object and manifests itself also? Does knowledge possess two different natures to manifest two different things, or does it manifest the object by the same nature by which it also manifests itself? As against these arguments, the Jainas could reply that the supposed infinite regress arises only if we accept either complete identity or complete difference. It does not arise if we accept the Jaina theory of *anekāntavāda*.

Are these two aspects non-different or different? If they are non-different then it cannot be decided whether they are the same or different from the knowledge whose aspects they are. If they are different, then it may be further asked, are they self-revealing or are they known by the knowledge whose aspects they are? In the first case, we have three self-revealing knowledges—the knowledge and its two aspects. Each one of these again will have two aspects insofar as it manifests itself and its object. This would lead to an infinite regress. On the second alternative, if the two aspects which are responsible for the manifestation of knowledge and of the object, are also objects of that knowledge, there would be another infinite regress. All these difficulties are avoided by the Jainas by holding that there is neither complete identity nor complete difference between the two aspects and the knowledge.[1]

1. *PKM*, p. 148.

(c) *The Bhāṭṭa View*

Kumārila regards knowledge as *not self-revealing* (*paraprakāśa*) in the sense of being "inferentially, known by some thing other than itself" (*para-anumeya*), for according to him knowledge is by nature non-perceptible (*parokṣa*) and is to be known by means of an inference. The *Bhāṭṭa* argument may be stated thus : Whatever is not given as an object (*karmatvena*) is not perceived. Knowledge can never be given as an object, therefore knowledge cannot be perceived. Even if knowledge is perceived, another knowledge would be required as the instrument for this perception. If this knowledge again is to be perceived then we shall need a third knowledge, and in this manner there would be an infinite regress. If the second knowledge can be an instrument without itself being perceived, then why cannot the first knowledge also do its job without being perceived. The *Bhāṭṭas* therefore hold that knowledge is not perceived at all. Knowledge is neither self-manifested nor directly perceived, but inferred from the character of "knowness" (*jñātatā*) in the object that has been known.

This argument is rejected by the Jainas on the ground[1] that the reason advanced by the *Bhāṭṭas* is not satisfactory, for although the self and the result of *pramāṇa* both are never given as objects yet they are directly perceived. The self is immediately perceived by every one. There can also be no doubt that the result of a *pramāṇa*, namely, the manifestation of the object, is directly perceived. If the Bhāṭṭas reply that these two cases are the only exception to the rule, since the self is perceived as *kartā* and the manifestation is perceived as result of knowledge (*pramāṇaphala*), then the Jainas would reply that the same exception can be made also in the case of knowledge which is given as *karaṇa* or an instrument.

The *Bhāṭṭas* have argued that knowledge is not directly known because it is not given as an object. The Jainas ask, what is meant by the *hetu* in this inference ? If knowledge cannot be an object for any *pramāṇa*, then the very existence of the knowledge cannot be established. It would be as fictitious as the horn of a hare. If knowledge becomes a fiction, then all objects of knowledge would become unreal, because the object

1. *SR*, I, p. 213.

of knowledge can be proved to be real only with the help of knowledge. Thus there would be *sarvaśūnyatāvāda* or universal nihilism.

It cannot be said that the nature of knowledge is such as it cannot be known, for the universal experience of mankind would contradict such a hypothesis. Everyone has the experience, 'I know'.

That knowledge is directly perceived may be proved in the following way. Whatever manifests an object as qualified by its own form is itself perceived, as for example the light of a lamp. Knowledge manifests its object as known. Therefore knowledge is directly perceived.[1]

5. *Nature of Object*

Regarding the nature of the object, five different views are found in Indian Philosophy:[2] (a) the view of absolute permanence (*kevala nityavāda*), (b) the view of absolute change (*kevala anityavāda*), (c) the view of the permanent which yet undergoes transformations (*pariṇāmīnityavāda*), (d) the view of both change and permanence (*nitya-anitya-ubhayavāda*), and (e) the view of permanence coupled with change (*nitya-anityātamakavāda*).

The *Advaita Vedāntists* accept the first view (the view of absolute permanence) because, according to them, change is mere appearance (*ābhāsamātra*). The Buddhists believe in the second view of absolute change for they are momentarists. The *Sāṁkhya* and *Yoga* schools accept the third view; they hold that every thing apart from conscious elements is a transformation of a permanent substance. According to the *Nyāya-Vaiśeṣikas*, certain entities are absolutely permanent and certain others absolutely changing. The Jainas hold that everything is permanent as well as changing. That is, a real entity is of the form of a substance and its modes, (*dravyaparyāyātmaka*) of the form of something permanent as well as changing. Hemacandra

1. yat svākāropahitam ākārāntaram upalambhayati tat parokṣaṁ na bhavati pratyakṣaṁ vā bhavati, yathā pradīpādyālokaḥ, upalambhayati ca jñānaṁ svākāropahitaṁ nīlādikamiti. *NKC*, p. 177.

2. Pt. Sukhalalji, *Advanced Studies in Indian Logic and Metaphysics*, p. 110.

rejects[1] the view of absolute permanence held by the *Vedāntists* and the view of absolute change held by the Buddhists, and defends logically the Jaina view of permanence coupled with change He defines the object of the knowledge as (*dravyaparyāyātmakaṁ vastu*) or reality is of the nature of something permanent as well as change. An object is both permanent and changing in the sense that its qualities and modes are in a process of change while the object is permanent. Thus, in respect of qualities the object is changing, and in respect of the object itself it is permanent. By accepting the view that the object is of the form of substance and its modes, the form of something permanent and something changing, Hemacandra rejects the view of the others who hold that the object is not permanent and changing at the same time or that the object is either absolutely permanent or absolutely changing.

The opponents ask, why cannot the object of knowledge be the substance only or the mode only or both the substance and modes separately? Hemacandra replies that the object which has the capacity to perform a function is the object of knowledge and such an object is of the nature of permanence and change *at once*. Only such an object which is both permanent and changing can have caused efficiency.[2]

Casual efficiency is the defining character of reality. Only that which can produce an effect is real.[3] And only such an object is known by a *pramāṇa*. It is only a person, who desires something, who takes recourse to a *pramāṇa*. Through a *pramāṇa* he determines the nature of an object and has his desires fulfilled. If the object of *pramāṇa* did not have casual efficiency then no one will take the help of *pramāṇa*. The substance without its modes cannot be able to perform the function. In order to reject the view of absolute permanence, he asks, if knowledge is only of the nature of permanence then how is it able to perform a function? Will it do it gradually or will it do it at once? It cannot be done gradually. If there is only the permanent substance, then there can be no change of the things. A merely permanent substance cannot produce its effect gradually, for

1. *PM*, I, 1.30.
2. *arthakriyāsāmarthyāt*. *Ibid.*, I,1.31.
3. *Ibid.*, I,1.32.

it should produce its effects in the very first moment. If it waits for some time to do it, then it really does not have the power to produce the effect. It may be replied that although the substance has the power it may still wait for the auxiliary (*sahakārī*) causes. But this is not a satisfactory answer, because what depends upon other factors for producing its effect does not really have the power. The dependent is powerless. The opponent might argue that it is not the substance which depends on the other factors, but it is the effect which waits for them. But Hemacandra does not accept this argument. If the cause has really the power then we cannot understand why it cannot produce the effect unless the other factors are present. Do the auxiliary factors produce in the cause some excellence (*upakāra*) or not? If they do not produce any *Upakāra* then the same problem remains. If they do produce some *Upakāra*, then we have to ask, whether the original cause is different or non-different from this *Upakāra*. If they are non-different, then the cause itself is produced by the auxiliary factors, which is absurd. If they are different, how can we say that this *Upakāra* belongs to that cause? It may be suggested that they may be different but related. But then the question is, what could be the relation between a cause and the *Upakāra* produced in it. The relation cannot be *saṁyoga*, for *saṁyoga* holds good between substances. It cannot be *samavāya*, for the Jainas do not accept the relation of *samavāya*.

Again, the permanent substance cannot produce its effect suddenly; because, all the effects cannot be seen as produced at once. If in the first moment all the effects are produced at once, then what would be done in the other moments? If the cause produces some effects in the second, third and other moments, then there would be the same difficulties as we have seen in the first case. If no effect is produced in the second moment then it would become unreal, for only that which produces is real. Thus a merely permanent substance cannot produce its effect, either gradually or all at once. Therefore, it does not have casual efficiency and it is not real.

On the other hand, the modes alone which are changing cannot produce effect gradually, because they are momentary and have no permanence in time and space. Due to permanence a function is performed in different times and spaces. The merely changing thing cannot do so.

The Buddhists might reply that though the momentary real cannot produce effect in succession, yet we can ascribe succession to a series; but Hemacandra, however, replies that a series is not real. If the series were real, we have to say whether it is momentary or not? If it is momentary, then the same difficulty as before arises. If it is not momentary, then we are giving up the theory that the real is only change.

The momentary real cannot produce its effect all at once. If a momentary cause produces two different effects, then these two effects being produced by the same nature of the cause would become identical. It may be suggested that the different effects are produced by different aspects of the cause. For example, some may be produced by the material cause and some by the auxiliary cause. To this suggestion we might ask, do these causes belong to the nature of the one momentary cause or do they not? If they do not belong to its nature then they cannot be said to be aspects of the same thing. If they belong to its nature then we have to ask, how these different aspects are compatible with the unity of the cause. Thus, the momentary real cannot produce effect either gradually or in succession. Therefore, it does not possess causal efficiency and so is not real.

The opponent may ask, even if the object is both *dravya* (substance) and *paryāya* (mode), how can it have the causal efficiency? They point out that an object, which is both *dravya* and *paryāya*, cannot produce its effects, either gradually or all at once. A real, even if it is both permanent and changing, cannot produce its effect gradually; for if it has the power then it cannot take time, it cannot also wait for auxiliary factors. The *paryāyas* being momentary cannot also produce effect in succession nor can the real produce effect all at once, for in that case it cannot exist in the next moment, because the same difficulties as before seem to arise even in the Jaina theory. This objection is answered by Hemacandra thus:

(i) The causal efficiency of such a real is explained by *pariṇāma* (result), whose nature consists in the preceding state giving up its form and the succeeding state taking a new form, though the substance remains the same.

(ii) Reality is neither mere *dravya* nor mere *paryāya*, nor does it consist of both *dravya* and *paryāya*. It is of a mixed character comprising of origination, destruction and permanence.[1] Such a real produces its effects either gradually, depending on auxiliary factors, or all at once. The auxiliary factors produce in it some *upakāra*, which is both different and non-different from the object. In this way all the objections are answered and Hemacandra concludes that the object of knowledge is reality, which is of the nature of both *dravya* and *paryāya*.

6. *The Classification of Knowledge*[2]

In the Jaina works, the knowledge is classified in two different ways—the *Āgamic* Classification and the logical classification. The *Āgamic* classification is older than the logical classification.

According to the *Āgamic* Classification the knowledge is classified in three different ways.

I) According to the first, the knowledge is divided into five types. In the *Bhagavatīsūtra*, knowledge is said to be of five types: (i) *ābhinibodhika*, (ii) *śruta*, (iii) *avadhi*, (iv) *manaḥparyāya* and (v) *kevala*. Th first two are sensuous knowledges and the later three are transcendental knowledges.

II) According to the second view, knowledge is divided mainly into two types, *pratyakṣa* and *parokṣa* and these two knowledges have been subdivided into five types. Under *pratyakṣa* come *kevala*, *avadhi* and *manaḥparyāya*; and under *parokṣa* come *ābhinibodhika* and *śruta*.
This classification is found in *Sthānāṅga-Sūtra*. Umāsvāti, in his *Tattvārthasūtra*, classified knowledge on this basis.

1. *kintu sthityutpādavyayātmakaṁ sabalaṁ jātyantarameva vastu. Ibid*, I, 1.33.
2. Malavaniya, *Āgamayuga Kā Jaina Darśana*, 127-147.

The Table of the Second Āgamic View

- Knowledge
  - *Pratyakṣa*
    - *Kevala*
    - *Avadhi*
    - *Manaḥparyāya*
  - *Parokṣa*
    - *Ābhinibodhika*
    - *Śruta*

III) The *Nandi-Sūtra* classifies knowledge in a different way. At first knowledge is divided into two types—*pratyakṣa* and *parokṣa*. The former is divided into five types of sensuous knowledge and three types of transcendental knowledge; and *parokṣa* is divided again into two types of sensuous knowledges.

The Table of the Third View

- *Knowledge*
  - *Pratyakṣa*
    - 1. *Śrotrendriya*
      2. *Cakṣu-indriya*
      3. *Ghrāṇendriya*
      4. *Jihvā-indriya*
      5. *Sparśendriya*
    - 1. *Avadhi*
      2. *Manaḥparyāya*
      3. *Kevala*
  - *Parokṣa*
    - *Ābhinibodhika*
    - *Śruta*

The main point of the *Āgamic* classification is that it does not come in under the influence of the theories of *pramāṇa*. Although knowledge is divided as *pratyakṣa* and *parokṣa*, yet the words *pratyakṣa* and *parokṣa* are used in different senses, not in the senses of the theories of *pramāṇa*. In the first *Āgamic* view, knowledge is classified only in five types. In the second *Āgamic* view, knowledge is at first divided in two types and then subdivided in five types. Here the word *pratyakṣa* denotes *direct knowledge* which arises directly by the power of the self without the help of the sense organs. And the word *parokṣa* denotes *indirect knowledge*, which arises with the help of the sense organs. These direct and indirect knowledges may be called as supersensuous or nonsensuous knowledges.

According to the third view, knowledge is divided into *pratyakṣa* and *parokṣa.* In this classification, the main point is this that the sensuous knowledge also comes under *pratyakṣa.* According to this view, *pratyakṣa* is of two types, the *indriya pratyakṣa* or the sensuous knowledge, and *anindriya pratyakṣa* or the transcendental knowledge. It seems that the third view of *Āgamic* classification is influenced by the other systems of Indian philosophy, because this classification accepts *pratyakṣa* as the sensuous knowledge as in the other systems. While in the second view of *Āgamic* classification, *pratyakṣa* is held as only transcendental knowledge. Nandikāra is the first amongst the Jainas to use *pratyakṣa* in the sense of sensuous knowledge. He divides *pratyakṣa* into two classes (i) the *indriya pratyakṣa* or the sensuous knowledge and (ii) *anindriya pratyakṣa* or the transcendental knowledge. The first is of five types and the second of three. These two types of *pratyakṣa* are accepted by the Jainas. Later on, these two are called *sāṁvyavahārika pratyakṣa* or sensuous perception and *mukhya pratyakṣa* or transcendental perception in the logical sense.[1]

1. *NKC,* I 3.

CHAPTER II

THE JAINA THEORY OF *PRAMĀṆA*

1. *Pramā and Pramāṇa*

In Indian philosophy, two words are used to stand for knowledge: *jñāna* and *pramā*. *jñāna* means all kinds of knowledge, true or false. But the word *pramā* is used only in the sense of true knowledge or *yathārtha jñāna*. True knowledge or *yathārtha jñāna* is distinct from false knowledge. In other words, the word *jñāna* is used for knowledge from the psychological standpoint; knowledge or *jñāna* is taken to mean any cognition of an object, while the word *pramā* is used in the logical sense. The *pramā* means right or true knowledge of an object. Thus in the logical sense knowledge is that which is true. And a knowledge is true when it represents its object with that nature and character which belong to it. All philosophers accept *pramā* in the sense of valid knowledge but they hold different views as regards the meaning of validity or truth of knowledge. For example, the *Naiyāyikas* regard true knowledge or *pramā* as true presentational knowledge. The Buddhists hold that the truth of knowledge (*yathārthānubhava*), consists in its practical value. According to the *Advaita Vedāntists*, the truth of knowledge consists in its non-contradictoriness. The *Mimāṁsakas* hold that the truth of knowledge consists in non-contradictoriness, i.e., *pramā* is defined as uncontradicted knowledge whose object was not known before (*anadhigata*). According to the Jainas, judgmental knowledge which is other than doubt, error, etc., is true knowledge or *pramā*. In other words, right judgment about an object is *pramā*.[1]

The special source of *pramā* or valid knowledge is called *pramāṇa*. *Pramāṇa* is defined as the *karaṇa* or the extraordinary cause of a *pramā* or right knowledge. Generally speaking, we may say that *pramāṇa* is the means of right knowledge. It is that which gives us right knowledge of object. Though all accept *pramāṇa* as the *karaṇa* or the extraordinary means of

1. *PM*, p. 3.

pramā yet there are differences of opinion about the characteristics of *karaṇa* or *pramāṇa*. Thus the philosophers have different views regarding the nature of *pramāṇa*.

The older *Naiyāyikas* define *pramāṇa* as the cause of an apprehension of object (*upalabdhihetupramāṇam*).[1] The Buddhist define *pramāṇa* as uncontradicted experience (*pramāṇam avisaṁvādijñānam*).[2] According to the *Bhāṭṭas*, *pramāṇa* is that which gives us new knowledge, i.e., a true knowledge of objects of which we have had no knowledge in the past (*anadhigatārthābhūtārthaniścayātmakaṁ pramāṇam*).[3] According to the *Sāṁkhya*, mental modification is *pramāṇa*, the self knows an object through a mental modification (*buddhi-vṛtti*).

Generally the Jainas define *pramāṇa* as knowledge which reveals itself and its object, and which must be determinate (*sva-para-vyavasāyijñānaṁ pramāṇam*)[4]. It is the definition of *pramāṇa* commonly given by the Jaina logicians. But the different logicians of different times have also defined *pramāṇa* in their own ways. Though the definitions are different, yet their meanings are not very different. The first great logician, Siddhasena defines *pramāṇa* as, "knowledge which is self-revealing and object-revealing and which is free from contradictions".[5] Akalaṅka, the systematizer of Jaina logic, defines *pramāṇa* by using the adjective *anadhigata* (unknown) for the object of *pramāṇa*, i.e., "*pramāṇa* is knowledge which is uncontradicted and which manifests the unknown object".[6] Māṇikyanandī, a follower of Akalaṅka, defines *pramāṇa* by using the word *apūrva* in the same sense as Akalaṅka. But he has used also the other adjective *sva* which had come from Siddhasena.

Thus Māṇikyanandi defines *pramāṇa* as the knowledge which reveals itself and the unknown object and which is "determinate".[7]

Vidyānandi and Vādidevasūri define *pramāṇa* in another

1. *NB*, p. 226.
2. *PVT*, I,3.
3. *SD*, p. 123.
4. *PNT*, I,2.
5. *pramāṇaṁ sva-parābhāsi bādhāvivarjitam. NAV*, I,2.
6. *pramāṇam avisaṁvādijñānam anadhigatārthādhigamalakṣaṇatvāt. AS*, p. 175.
7. *svāpūrvārthavyavasāyātmakaṁ jñānaṁ pramāṇam. PKM*, I.

way. They do not use word like *anadhigata, avisaṁvādi, apūrva*, etc. They simply define it as *svārthavyavasāyātmakaṁ jñānaṁ pramāṇam* or as '*sva-para-vyavasāyi jñānaṁ pramāṇam*'. According to Vidyānandi, *pramāṇa* is the knowledge which reveals itself and the object and it must be determinate (*vyavasāyātmakaṁ or vyavasāyi*). Since the object of *pramāṇa* may be known or unknown, the words *anadhigata* and *apūrva* as used by Akalaṅka and Māṇikyanandi are useless.[1] Hemacandra defines *pramāṇa*[2] as *saṁyogārthanirṇayapramāṇam*. It means that *pramāṇa* is the knowledge which possesses the property of truly determining the nature of object. The definition may also be stated in the form of an inference of the following form. "This knowledge truly determines the nature of its object, because it is a *pramāṇa*."

Artha is that which is an object of right knowledge. *Nirṇaya* means judgmental knowledge which is other than doubt, error etc. Though, they are knowledge yet they are not *pramāṇa*. The word *samyak* is the adjective of the word *nirṇaya*. *Samyak nirṇaya* means right judgment. To acquire true knowledge right judgment is necessary. The object itself is not right or wrong. Thus *samyak* means to be true of the object, or not to be contradictory of the object. Therefore, the definition excludes error.

The older Jaina philosophers, as we have described above, define *pramāṇa* by saying that knowledge is *pramāṇa*, which reveals itself and its object. Hemacandra accepts that knowledge is self-revealing, but he does not take it to be a definition of *pramāṇa*. Because this property of being self-revealing belongs to all knowledge, including the false ones. Therefore, he says that we cannot define a *pramāṇa* with the help of this property.

Again, pramāṇa is knowledge because it enables us to accept the acceptable (*upādeya*) things and to reject the things which are not acceptable (*heya*).[3] It has the power to lead to an acceptance or rejection of things, and so it must be of the nature of knowledge. There are two kinds of objects. They are either

1. *tad evārthavyavasāyātmajñānaṁ manyeta yathā, lakṣaṇena'gatārthatvād vyartham anyad* viśeṣaṇam, *TSV*, 77, p.174.

2. *PM*, I, 1.2.

3. *abhimatānabhimatavastusvīkāratiraskārakṣamaṁ hi pramāṇam atojñānamevedam. PNT*, I,3.

heya, i.e., an object of hatred, or *upādeya*, i.e., an object of desire. We get the sense of what object we should accept or what object we should reject due to knowledge. Knowledge alone possesses this capacity. Thus knowledge is *pramāṇa*. There is a third kind of object which is neither desirable nor undesirable but which is the object of indifference. One does not possess any kind of feeling towards such object. For example, walking on grass one is indifferent to the grass under one's feet. Even such *upekṣaṇīya* objects are manifested by *pramāṇa*.

Pramāṇa is knowledge, because it enables us to accept or reject an object. The manifestation of an object is due to the capacity of knowledge. In manifestation of knowledge neither the object comes to the agent nor the agent comes to the object. It is the knowledge itself which manifests the object.[1] Therefore, *pramāṇa* is knowledge, which is the extraordinary cause of the manifestation of an object. But when one actually gets his desired object, it is not due to the *pramāṇa* which manifests the object. In other words, at first knowledge manifests the object and the activity of getting the object depends on the knowledge. If there were no knowledge, there would be no activity directed towards the object. This may be seen in every day experience. The *prāpakatva* of a *pramāṇa* does not depend upon activity. When we see the sun or the moon, such knowledge may not give rise to any activity and yet the knowledge does manifest its object.

Since the *pramāṇa* is to be a knowledge which has the capacity for accepting or rejecting an object, nothing that is not knowledge, for example, the sense-object contact, can be called *pramāṇa*.

2. *Nyāya definition of Pramāṇa*

The older *Naiyāyikas* define *pramāṇa* as the cause of our apprehension of object (*upalabdhihetupramāṇa*).[2] Hemacandra asks, what is meant by the 'cause' here ? If all causes are meant, then even the object of knowledge and the subject of knowledge would become *pramāṇa*, for they also are amongst the causes of a knowledge. Therefore, by causes is meant not all causes but *karaṇa*, i.e., a special cause which being present the effect

1. *PNT*, 1.3.
2. *NB*, p. 226.

immediately follows. But the Jainas point out that according to this definition of *Karaṇa*, the contact of the senses with the object cannot be the *karaṇa*, for it does not immediately give rise to *upalabdhi*. What immediately causes *upalabdhi* is knowledge. Therefore, only knowledge deserves to be called *pramāṇa*. Only knowledge is conscious, the contact is non-conscious; therefore, it cannot manifest itself. What is not able to manifest itself cannot manifest an object: for example, a jar. Therefore, sense-object contact cannot by itself manifest an object.[1]

According to the *Nyāya* view, there are six kinds of *sannikarṣa* or sense object contact[2]:—*saṁyoga*, *saṁyukta-samavāya*, *saṁyukta-samaveta-samavāya*, *samavāya*, *samaveta-samavāya* and *viśeṣyaviśeṣaṇabhāva*. In all perceptual knowledge, sense object contact is necessary. But the Jainas refute this view; they say that *sannikarṣa* is not the extra-ordinary cause of knowledge. They point out that in many cases there is *sannikarṣa* but knowledge does not arise. For example, eye being *aprāpyakārī*, there cannot be *saṁyoga sambandha* between a jar and the eye. And if there is no *saṁyoga-sambandha*, there would be no other *sambandhas* as well. The *saṁyukta-samavāya-sambandha*, due to which the eye is supposed to apprehend the qualities of the object, is not able to produce knowledge in many cases. For example, the eye cannot apprehend the test of the object. In the same way, by *saṁyukta-samaveta-samavāya-sambandha* the eye cannot apprehend *rasatva* of the *rasa* belonging to a mango. By *samavāya* also the *mahatparimāṇa* etc., which are qualities of *ākāśa* (ether) cannot be apprehended by the ears. In the same way, in *samaveta-samavāya*, the *mahatparimāṇatva*, which inheres in a quality of *ākāśa*, is not apprehended by the eye. The sixth kind of sense object contact, i.e., the *viśeṣyaviśeṣaṇabhāva* is also refuted by other kinds of *sannikarṣa*. Thus, the Jainas say that all the six kinds of sense-object-contact may or may not produce knowledge; therefore they cannot be regarded as *karaṇa*.

The *Naiyāyikas* may reply to the above objection by saying that sense-object-contact can produce a knowledge only when it has the *yogyatā* (capacity) to produce it. The Jainas reject

1. *PM*, I,1.8.
2. *NM*, p. 68.

this answer, for if it is the *yogyatā* which causes a knowledge, then sense-object-contact is not the *karaṇa* at all.[1]

3. *Jayanta's Theory of Pramāṇa*

Like all other *Naiyāyikas*, Jayanta defines *pramāṇa* as the extraordinary cause of right knowledge. But *pramāṇa*, according to him, is not a single thing; it is a complex whole comprising of many conditions, just as the senses, the object, the agent, and the sense-object-contact. This complex whole is called *pramāṇa*. He defines it as "the complex of all the conscious and non-conscious conditions that are operative in bringing about a valid knowledge of objects."[2]

Thus the totality of conditions or *sāmagrī* is the extra-ordinary cause or *karaṇa* of right knowledge, for in the absence of any one of these conditions there is no right knowledge. All the conditions are necessary for right knowledge. Not only the *sāmagrī* is necessary for right knowledge but there is *avinābhāva* relation also between the result of knowledge and the *sāmagrī*; in other words, the result of knowledge depends on the *sāmagrī*.

Though the conditions or *sāmagrī* seem different, yet they, as combined together, are one. Any on e factor by itself is not able to produce knowledge. They are one in the sense of together producing knowledge.

The Jainas do not believe in the theory of *kārakasākalyavāda*. They hold that the *sāmagrī* is not the extraordinary cause of right knowledge. They define extraordinary cause as that which is immediately followed by the effect. The manifestation of the object follows immediately upon knowledge, but not upon the sense, the object and their contact. Extraordinary cause is that which being present the effect follows, and that which being absent the effect is absent. Thus knowledge is the extraordinary cause. The manifestation of an object depends on knowledge, not on the other factors. Without knowledge an object cannot be manifested, even when all the other factors are present. If knowledge were absent its effect would be absent. Thus knowledge alone is the extraordinary cause.[3]

1. *PKM*, pp. 15-16.
2. *avyabhicāriṇīmasandigdhāmarthopalabdhiṁ vidadhatī bodhābodhasvabhāvasāmagrī pramāṇam. NM*, p. 12.
3. *SR*, I,4.

According to the Jainas, *pramāṇa* is knowledge, which reveals both itself and the object. But *sāmagrī* is not of that nature; it cannot reveal itself; therefore, it cannot reveal the object, and so it is not the extraordinary cause of such revelation.[1]

Again, according to *kārakasākalyavāda*, the *sāmagrī* is both conscious and non-conscious (*bodhābodhasvabhāvā hi sāmagrī*).[2] The factors producing knowledge are of both kinds: some are conscious and some are non-conscious. The Jainas reject this view on the ground that the things which are non-conscious cannot produce knowledge. Although they are the secondary causes for producing knowledge, they are not the extraordinary causes of it. An object is manifested by knowledge, not merely by the *sāmagrī*. If there is no knowledge the *sāmagrī* alone cannot manifest an object. Therefore, not *sāmagrī* but knowledge alone is the *karaṇa*.

Jayanta holds that a *sāmagrī* cannot be there without producing effect. Now what is meant by this? Is it like the smoke which cannot exist without fire; or is it that the *sāmagrī* cannot be actualised without producing effect just as *śiṁśapātva* cannot be actualised in the absence of *vṛkṣatva*? Or, is it meant that the *sāmagrī* cannot exist without producing effect, just as a dark cloud cannot exist without producing rain? The first alternative is not true, because it involves circularity, for the result can follow only from *sāmagrī*, and the *sāmagrī* can exist only when there is the result. The second alternative cannot also be accepted, for like *śiṁśāpatva* and *vṛkṣatva*, the *sāmagrī* and its result are not simultaneously there. If we accept the third alternative, then it may be asked, does the *sāmagrī* produce the effect immediately or after sometimes? The first is not true, for the *sāmagrī* alone cannot manifest the object unless there is knowledge. As regards the second alternative, the *sāmagrī* cannot be said to be the extraordinary cause in the primary sense. It can be so only in a secondary sense.[3]

1. *na vai sannikarṣāderjñānasya prāmāṇyam upapannam, tasyārthāntarasyeva svārthavyavasitau sādhakatamatvānupapatteḥ. SR*, I, 4.
2. *Ibid.*
3. *Ibid.*

4. *The Sāṁkhya Theory of Pramāṇa*

According to the *Sāṁkhya*, the modification of *buddhi* or intellect is *pramāṇa*, because it conceptualises the object, which has been apprehended by the senses and mind. The Jainas reject this view, and hold that there is no perceptual knowledge of the modification of the senses and mind. How could senses be modified by the object ? It cannot also be known by inference, for there is no mark on which such an inference can be based. The *Sāṁkhya* philosopher may reply that there is a mark with which we could infer that the sense organs are modified by their objects; this mark is the fact that each sense organ can apprehend only some definite object and not another. The Jainas however would point out that this fact can be explained if we assume that each sense organ has the *yogyatā* to apprehend a certain kind of object.

Again, the Jainas point out that the *vṛtti* or modification, either of the senses or the mind or the *buddhi*, cannot produce knowledge by itself because it is by nature non-conscious.[1] Nobody can accept that the means for producing right knowledge could be non-conscious. Thus the *Vṛtti* is not *pramāṇa*. The *Sāṁkhya* may reply that though the senses, mind, and *buddhi* are non-conscious and their *vṛtti* cannot manifest the object yet due to the reflection of the *puruṣa* or consciousness on it, it can manifest the object. The Jainas reject this argument by saying that if it be said that the *vṛtti* produces knowledge due to the reflection of *puruṣa* or consciousness, then it is better to say that the *puruṣa* or the self is *pramāṇa*. It is the self that has the cognition of object and not any *vṛtti* or modification of non-conscious instruments.

Again, if the *vṛtti* or modification of *buddhi* is *pramāṇa*, then what is the relation between the *buddhi* and its *vṛtti* ? Are they different or non-different ? If they are non- different then there is no difference between *buddhi* and its *vṛtti*; they would be identical and the *vṛtti* can also be called *buddhi*. But in that case, in sleep also one should have knowledge, for the *buddhi* is present in that state.

If the *vṛtti* and *buddhi* are different, then what is the relation

1. *SR*, I, p. 54.

between them? If they are non-different, then how can the senses grasp the object? If they are different and related by some other relation, then no such relation is accepted by the *Sāṁkhya*, because the *Sāṁkhya* does not accept any relation, such as *samavāya*, *saṁyoga* etc., other than the 25 *tattvas*.

The Jainas point out that the *vṛtti* of mind cannot also be *pramāṇa*, because mind also cannot apprehend the external objects by itself.[1]

5. *The Buddhist Definition of Pramāṇa*

The Buddhists define *pramāṇa* as the knowledge which is *avisaṁvādi*, i.e., not contradictory. But what do the Buddhists mean by knowledge? If they mean *nirvikalpa* knowledge, then it cannot be *pramāṇa*, for it does not give rise to *vyavahāra*. How then can the Buddhists hold that the *nirvikalpa* is *pramāṇa*. It cannot be said that *nirvikalpa* gives rise to *savikalpa* and the latter gives rise to *vyavahāra*, for it is better in that case to hold that the *savikalpa* is the *pramāṇa*. The Bauddhas, however, do not regard the *savikalpa* as *pramāṇa*. How then can they explain the fact that the *vyavahāra* caused by a *savikalpa* knowledge could be uncontradicted or *avisaṁvādi*; therefore according to Hemacandra, *savikalpa* is *pramāṇa*.[2]

6. *The Bhāṭṭa Definition of Pramāṇa*

According to the *Bhāṭṭa Mīmāṁsakas*, *pramāṇa* is that which gives us new knowledge, i.e., the object of the *pramāṇa* must not have been known before. It must be a new object. Vādideva asks, what is meant by saying that the object of the *pramāṇa* must not be known before? Is it not to be known by one and the same self or by any other person? If the object of a *pramāṇa* should not be known previously by any one else, then since all objects are known by the omniscient person, no ordinary knowledge would be a *pramāṇa*. And the knowledge of one person would not be right for the other person. If new knowledge alone is *pramāṇa* then it is not possible even in the case of the person himself. It is not a part of the meaning of 'truth' that its object should be different from what is already known. A

1. *SR*, I, p. 54.
2. *PM*, I, 1.8.

person may very well know truly what he already knows. The *Mīmāṁsakas* may ask, what is the function of *pramāṇa* in this case if the object is already known? To this the Jainas reply that it has the same function, as in the case when the object is previously unknown. The function is the destruction of ignorance. Further, it is not necessary that a *pramāṇa* should have a purpose. When all the conditions necessary for it are present, the *pramāṇa* arises. Therefore, even if the object is already known, if the conditions for it are present, then there may be again a true knowledge of it.[1]

1. *SR*, I.

CHAPTER III

THE JAINA THEORY OF PERCEPTION

1. *Meaning of Pratyakṣa*

According to the Jainas, the word *pratyakṣa* is derived from the word *akṣa*. *Akṣa* here means the self or *jīva*, that knows all objects in space and time.[1] But all the other systems of Indian philosophy mean by the word *akṣa indriya* or sense organ, and thus they understand by *pratyakṣa* the knowledge which is derived from the sense organs.[2]

Thus according to the early Jaina philosophers, the knowledge which is derived from the self is *pratyakṣa* and knowledge which does not arise from the self alone is called *parokṣa*[3]; in this sense, the sensuous knowledge (or the *indriya jñāna*) is not *pratyakṣa*. But later on, the Jaina philosophers came to accept the knowledge produced by the sense organs also as *pratyakṣa*. Thus, Jinabhadra and Akalaṅka designated it as *sāṁvyavahārika pratyakṣa*, while the real *pratyakṣa* of the *Āgamas* was called *pāramārthika pratyakṣa* or *mukhya pratyakṣa*. Subsequently, the Jaina philosophers accepted this classification of *pratyakṣa*. Thus, according to this classification, there are two types of *pratyakṣa*—the *sāṁvyavahārika* and the *mukhya*, or the empirical perception and the non-sensuous perception.

Hemacandra in his *Pramāṇa Mīmāṁsā* says that *akṣa* means either the self (that which knows everything)[4] or the sense organ (that which apprehends objects).[5] The *pratyakṣa*, therefore, means either the knowledge which arises from the self alone, or that which arises depending on the sense organs. The former is *mukhya pratyakṣa* or, litterally, superior perception which may be called non-sensuous perception, and the latter is *sāṁvyavahārika pratyakṣa* which may be called sense perception.

1. *akṣṇoti vyāpṇoti jānāti iti akṣa ātmā. SS*, I,12.
2. *akṣasyā'kṣasya prativiṣayaṁ vṛttiḥ pratyakṣam, NB*, I.1.3.
3. *TS*, I.12.
4. *aśnute aśnoti vā yvāpnoti sakaladravyakṣetrakālabhāvān iti akṣo jīvaḥ. PM*, I,1.10.
5. *aśnute viṣayam iti akṣam indriyaṁ ca. Ibid.*

2. *The Definition of Perception*

The Jaina logicians define perception as clear knowledge. Clarity is its specific quality. Thus Akalaṅka says, *pratyakṣaṁ viśadam.*[1] According to Vidyānandi, *pratyakṣa* is knowledge which is clear. Māṇikyanandi, Vādideva and Hemacandra also hold perception as clear knowledge.[2] Thus according to the Jainas perception is clear knowledge. Though all the scholars define it as clear knowledge, yet they explain this definition in different ways. They also examine the definitions of perception given in the other systems. Now we will explain the different explanations of perception given by different Jaina scholars.

(a) *Akalaṅka's definition*

Akalaṅka defines perception in his *Nyāyaviniścaya* thus: "Perception is the knowledge, which is self revealing and which reveals the object as substance and as mode, as universal and as particular, and which is determinate or conceptual and which is essentially clear."[3] Akalaṅka uses many adjectives in this definition. The commentator Vādirāja explains this definition in *Nyāyaviniścaya Vivaraṇa.* He explains all these adjectives one by one and we give below his explanations of Akalaṅka's definition.

At first, *pratyakṣa* is the knowledge which is self-revealing (*ātmavedanam*). As mentioned before, all knowledge, according to the Jainas, is self-revealing. Therefore, *pratyakṣa* is also self-revealing. If knowledge were not self-revealing it could not reveal its object. Therefore Akalaṅka uses the adjective self-revealing (*ātmavedanam*) for perception.

The next adjective is *that which reveals the object* (*artha*). Perception, like all knowledge, reveals its object. But the object of perception is *dravyaparyāyātmakam*, i.e., perception reveals its object with the aspects of substance and mode. For example, the object 'gold' is revealed in perception. Perception not

1. *NKC*, I,3.
2. *viśadaṁ pratyakṣam, PKM*; *spaṣṭaṁ pratyakṣaṁ, PNT*; *viśadaṁ pratyakṣaṁ, PM.*
3. *pratyakṣalakṣaṇaṁ prāhuḥ spaṣṭaṁ sākāramañjaśā / dravya-paryāya-sāmānya-viśeṣārthātmavedanam // NVV*, I.3.

only reveals the object as substance (*dravya*) 'gold' but also it apprehends the gold with its modes (*paryāya*), for the gold may have the form of a ring or of a chain. According to the Jainas, every object is the combination of substance and modes; substance is the permanent entity while modes are changing. Again, the object of perception possesses the universal and particular properties (*sāmānya-viśeṣa*). According to the Jainas, every object is *sāmānya-viśeṣātmaka*, i.e., every object has the universal and particular properties. For example, cowness is the universal property and 'black' or 'white' is a particular property of a cow. Similarity amongst the objects is due to their universal properties and their differences are due to particular properties. Thus, every object is *dravya paryāyātmaka* and *sāmānya-viśeṣātmaka*; and perception is the knowledge which apprehends such an object.

Again, Akalaṅka holds that perception is *sākāra-jñāna*. He gives this adjective in the sense of conceptual knowledge. Perception is conceptual knowledge; it is not non-conceptual or *kalpanāpoḍham* as the Buddhists hold. Perception is *sākāra* or conceptual in this sense that it has the power to manifest the object through concepts; it is not merely the pure sensation of unique individuals. Thus, perception manifests the object with all its qualities. Therefore, it is conceptual. It may be noted here that the Jainas regard all knowledge as *nirākāra* as against the Buddhists who regard knowledge as *sākāra*. But here when Akalaṅka defines perception as *sākāra*, he means it *savikalpaka* or conceptual perception.[1]

Further, Akalaṅka adds that perception is clear (*viśada*) knowledge. The opponent may ask, what is meant by 'clear' in this definition? Does it mean direct apprehension (*sākṣāt-karaṇam*) of the object? But the meaning of 'direct apprehension' is equally difficult to explain.[2]

Direct apprehension is not that which is caused, e.g., by light, because light may be a cause of inference also; as for example, the inference of fire may be based on the light of

1. *pratyakṣaṁ savikalpena jainasya, yadāha sākāram iti savikalpam* ca nāma jātyādiviṣayatvam, *NVV*, p. 86.

2. *Kīdṛśaṁ spaṣṭam iti sākṣātakaraṇam iti cet; tadapi durbodhanam. Ibid*, p. 85.

fire itself. Again, in some cases there is no light but there may be direct apprehension as in the case of the apprehension of taste.[1]

If 'direct apprehension' is taken to mean the knowledge which apprehends the object without any interference, then that also is not acceptable, because in some cases an object may be directly apprehended, even if there is the interference by something. For example, an object which is in a glass jar is directly apprehended although it is covered with the glass.[2]

Further, does 'direct apprehension' mean the apprehension of the true nature of the object (*vastusvarūpagrahaṇam*)? No, for this is possible in inference also.

Does 'direct apprehension' mean knowledge without doubt, error etc.? Vādirāja replies that this is not so, because in the case of inference also the knowledge is free from doubt or error.[3]

Akalaṅka says that 'direct knowledge' means clear knowledge. Perception is clear knowledge, the knowledge which is not based on any other knowledge, unlike inference and verbal knowledge. Perception manifests its object without the mediation of any other knowledge, therefore it is clear knowledge. What is not clear, is not perception, just as inference.[4]

The opponents may ask, what is meant by the word *pratyakṣa*? According to them, *akṣa* means the sense organs, and the knowledge derived form the sense organs is called *pratyakṣa*. The Jainas point out that if *pratyakṣa* means the knowledge produced by the sense organs, then the mental perception and non-sensuous perception could not be called *pratyakṣa*. The Jainas hold, as stated earlier that *akṣa* means the *jīva* or the self, which knows itself and the object, and knowledge produced by the *akṣa* or the self is called *pratyakṣa*.

But Akalaṅka holds that sense knowledge may also be called *pratyakṣa* in the secondary sense. The sense organs are of the nature of consciousness, which is the power, received from the self. Therefore, the knowledge produced by the sense organs may also be called *pratyakṣa*.[5] Thus, *pratyakṣa* is clear knowledge; it

1. *NVV*, p. 85.
2. *Ibid.*
3. *Ibid.*
4. *Ibid.*, p. 95.
5. *Ibid.*

is produced either by the soul or by the sense organs. The word *añjasā* may be explained, either as quality of being *viśada* or as quality of being *sākāra*. In fact, the commentator Vādirāja explains it in both ways. In the first case, it would mean that clarity is its (i.e., perception's) essential quality. That is perception is a clear knowledge; it is clear by its own nature (*añjasā*).[1]

In the second sense, the word *añjasā* is used as the adjective of *sākāra*. Knowledge is *añjasā sākāra*, i.e., *sākāra* is the essential quality of knowledge.[2] Perception is really *sākāra*.

Akalaṅka defines perception as knowledge which reveals itself and the object as substance and mode; the knowledge is essentially *sākāra* or conceptual and is also essentially clear or direct knowledge. Here the important point is that all the adjectives used by Akalaṅka are not merely of *pratyakṣa* or of perception but some of them are true of all knowledge. All knowledge, whether perceptual (*pratyakṣa*) or non-perceptual (*parokṣa*), is self-revealing, object-revealing and conceptual. But the adjectives *viśada* and *añjasā* are used only for the *pratyakṣa*.[3] All knowledge is not clear essentially; only perception is clear, for it is not based on other knowledges; whereas other knowledges, like inference and verbal knowledge, are dependent on some other knowledge. Here the Nyāya definition of perception as *jñānakaraṇakaṁ jñānaṁ pratyakṣam* may be compared with Akalaṅka's definition of *pratyakṣa* as clear knowledge. Both define perception as a knowledge which is not brought about by the instrumentality of any other knowledge.

(b) *Māṇikyanandi's Definition*

Māṇikyanandi defines perception in the *sūtra*: 'clear knowledge is *pratyakṣa*.[4] Prabhācandra explains the definition thus: clear knowledge is called *pratyakṣa*. Whatever is not clear knowledge, cannot be called *pratyakṣa*, just as inference. The Buddhist might contend that where there is an inference of fire immediately after seeing smoke the knowledge is really perceptual. Again, even *vyāptijñāna* may be regarded as percep-

1. *pratyakṣalakṣaṇaṁ prāhusspaṣṭamañjasā iti. NVV*, p. 98.
2. *aṅjasā paramārthata eva sākāraṁ kalpayet, Ibid*. p. 103.
3. *pratyakṣalakṣaṇaṁ prāhusspaṣṭamañjasā. Ibid*. p. 98.
4. *viśadaṁ pratyakṣaṁ. PKM*, II,3.

tual. But from the above definition it follows that these are not perceptions because they are *aspaṣṭa* or unclear knowledges, whereas perception is *spaṣṭa* or clear.

The Jainas point out that the *vyāpti-jñāna* like 'wherever there is smoke there is fire' is not clear knowledge, therefore this also is not *pratyakṣa*.[1] The question may arise, whether the *vyāpti-jñāna* is knowledge of *sāmānya* or of *viśeṣa*. If the knowledge is of *sāmānya*, then it is not *pratyakṣa*, because according to the Buddhists, *sāmānya* is not an object of perception. If it be said that the *sāmānya* can be an object of perception, then the Buddhists have to contradict their own thesis that corresponding to the two *pramāṇas* there are two *prameyas*.

If what is known in inference be not the *sāmānya* firehood, but a particular fire, then there ought not to be doubt in the mind of the person who is inferring whether this fire is a grass fire or a fire from the leaves. When one perceives fire close by, then he will not have any such doubt. Where such doubt arises the knowledge must be either from *śabda* or from a mark. It is not perceptual.[2]

If the *vyāpti jñāna* were clear, i.e., if we know all smokes and all fires clearly, then nothing would be left for inference to know. Therefore, inference will become useless. We do not experience a clear perception of all smokes and all fires. Therefore, *vyāptijñāna* is not perception.[3]

Thus, if the knowledge is not clear, then it is not perception. Now, is this vagueness (*aspaṣṭatā*) a quality of the knowledge or of the object ?[4] If it is a quality of the knowledge, then how can the object of knowledge be called vague ? The quality of one thing does not belong to the other; there is no such rule that if one thing is not clear the other also would not be clear. If vagueness is the quality of the object, then the *vyāptijñāna* cannot be proved to be non-perceptual. The same difficulty arises in the case of clearness also. According to Prabhācandra clearness and vagueness are properties of knowledge, and not

1. *PKM*, II. p. 216.
2. *Ibid.*
3. *Ibid*, p. 217.
4. *Ibid.*

properties of object. There is no fault if the properties of knowledge are transferred to the object.[1]

What is the cause of the clarity of knowledge ? It is well-known that the clarity of knowledge is due to removal of obstruction, which in the present case, is the *karmic* matter. The concept of *karmic* matter will be explained later in Part III.

The *Mīmāṁsakas* hold that the clarity of knowledge is due to the sense organs; but according to the Jainas, the destruction of the *āvaraṇa* or the veil of *karmic* matter is the cause of clarity since the sense organs are not the causes of clarity.[2]

Further, what is meant in the definition by the clarity of knowledge ? Māṇikyanandi says in the next *sūtra* that perpetual knowledge is clear in the sense that there is no mediation of any other knowledge or *pramāṇa* in knowing the object. A knowledge is clear when it does not require any other knowledge in order to manifest its object.[3] Inference is not clear knowledge because it is based on other knowledges, including the *vyāpti jñāna*; but *pratyakṣa* is clear in the sense that it is not based on any other knowledge to manifest its object. But immediately and distinctly it manifests its object without the mediation of any other *pramāṇa*. Here, we may compare the *Nyāya* definition of perception which holds that "perception is knowledge which is not brought about by the instrumentality of any antecedent knowledge (*jñānakaraṇakaṁ jñānaṁ pratyakṣam*)."[4]

The opponent may point out that this is not true because there is in perceptual knowledge the mediation of such knowledges as *avagraha*, *īhā*, *avāya* etc.,[5] and therefore it cannot be called clear in the above sense. To this objection, Prabhācandra replies that *avagraha*, *īhā* etc., are not different kinds of knowledge but the stages of the one process of perceptual knowledge. The process of perception passes through these four stages, and they are not totally different, they come one after another. They are not different knowledges because they have the same object and subject. Therefore, there is no mediation of another

1. *PKM*, p. 217.
2. *Ibid*, p. 219.
3. *pratītyantarāvyavadhānena viśeṣavṛttyā vā pratibhāsanaṁ vaiśadyam*, *Ibid.*
4. Chatterjee, S.C., *The Nyāya Theory of Knowledge*, p. 127.
5. These will be discussed later on, in Ch. V.

knowledge in perceptual knowledge, and so this knowledge is clear in the above sense.

Again, clarity is the special quality of perception although in some cases the object of it may not be clear. In darkness, for example, one cannot see an object clearly. But even in such case, we do perceive the generic feature (*saṁsthāna*), while the specific features, i.e., whether the object is a man or tree are inferred. As one approaches an object nearer and nearer, more and more of its specific qualities may come to be perceived.[1]

(c) *Hemacandra's Definition*

Hemacandra defines *Pratyakṣa* as clear knowledge. Clarity is its special quality, that is, direct knowledge or *Pratyakṣa* means clear knowledge.[2] The *Pratyakṣa* may also be defined in the form of an inference thus: "This perception is a clear and true knowledge of its object, because it is perceptual knowledge; if there is no clarity in knowledge, then there is on direct knowledge, as in the case of *parokṣa* knowledge."

Now, what is meant by clarity or *vaiśadya*? If it is called clear because it apprehends its objects then *parokṣa* or indirect knowledge would also be clear because they also apprehend their objects. If it is clear in the sense of being self-revealing then all knowledge is self-revealing and would be clear.

In view of these difficulties, Hemacandra defines 'clarity' in the next *sūtra*.[3] He gives two explanations. In the first place, perception is clear in the sense that it is not dependent as any other knowledge, such as verbal knowledge and inference. Secondly, it is clear in the sense that its object is manifested as a "this". Thus Hemacandra gives us two definitions of clarity. Thereby we get two important features of perception. It does not depend upon any other knowledge, and it always apprehends its object as something *given here and now* with its specific qualities and not merely in its generic character. Thus, Hemacandra follows, in this respect, Māṇikyanandi and Prabhā-

1. *PKM*, p. 220.
2. *viśadam pratyakṣam*. *PM*, I,1.13.
3. *pramāṇāntarānapekṣedaṁtayā* pratibhāso vā vaiśadyam. *Ibid*, I,1.14.

candra. Māṇikyanandi had also earlier defined *vaiśadya* in two ways.

3. *Criticism of the Buddhist definition of Perception*

According to the Buddhists, perception is non-conceptual knowledge or it is free from any concept. They define it as *pratyakṣaṁ kalpanā'poḍham.* Perception is a pure sensation, because its object is unique, momentary particulars, without name, class etc. In perceptual knowledge, at first there is pure sensation of the unique individuals, then the concept; but there would be a lapse of time between the sensation and its concept. In the meantime, the object also would change, for it is momentary; therefore, they hold that the conceptual knowledge cannot be right knowledge, because it has to be based on the memory of the sensed object. Perception is true as mere sensation, if it has any concept it would be false. Thus they define perception as true knowledge, free from any concept. All conceptual knowledge is false according to them, because they are based on the memory of the object, not on the real object.

According to Akalaṅka, the so-called *avikalpaka* perception is not really perception but only appears to be perception (*pratyakṣābham*).[1] Why should such an *avikalpaka* knowledge be called perception ? *Avikalpaka* knowledge cannot be a cause of action (*pravṛtti*), for all *pravṛtti* is caused by *a savikalpaka* or conceptual knowledge.

According to Akalaṅka, the only valid perception is that which is conceptual or judgemental (*paṭīyasāmavisaṁvādaniyamāt*).[2]

It may be asked, if there is no *avikalpaka* perception at all, then why does Akalaṅka say that it is not perception but appears to be perception ? To this the commentator Vādirāja replies that the *avikalpaka*, about which Akalaṅka speaks, is not what he regards as real, but is what the Buddhists talk about.[3]

Akalaṅka goes on in the next *sūtra* 154, to point out that the Buddhist view that all *vikalpa* or concept is false cannot be

1. *NVV*, I,158.
2. *Ibid.*
3. *avikalpasya pratyakṣābhatvacintanaṁ tu parā'bhigamaprasiddhasyaiva na vastubalapravṛttasya. Ibid*, p. 521.

accepted. Vādirāja in his explanation of this passage asks the question, is the falsity of all *vikalpa* known *svataḥ or parataḥ* ? He shows that none of these alternatives is acceptable. If falsity of *vikalpa* is known as *svataḥ* then in the case of knowledge like "this is blue", truth also should be known as *svataḥ*. Further, if the falsity of all *vikalpa* is known as *svataḥ*, then why do the Buddhists make use of inference to prove their thesis ? It is not also apprehended *parataḥ*. It cannot be apprehended by a *nirvikalpaka* perception or non-conceptual perception, for *nirvikalpaka* does not apprehend *vikalpa* nor can it be apprehended by some other *vikalpa*, because all *vikalpas* or concepts, according to the Buddhists, are false.

Again, if *vikalpa* is false, then the Buddhists cannot use *vikalpa* to prove that *pratyakṣa* is a *pramāṇa*.[1] But they still try to establish *pratyakṣa* as a *pramāṇa*. They cannot use also an inference, which is a form of *vikalpa*, to prove the existence of *nirvikalpa* perception. But they do use such inference.[2] Akalaṅka says, therefore, that the Buddhist view that all *vikalpa* is false, is absurd.

4. *Buddhist View of Mental Perception*

According to the Buddhists, mental perception is a knowledge which arises immediately after sense perception. Its object is that which arises in the next moment after the objects of sense perception and which belongs to the same series. The object of the sense perception is momentary and so does not last up to the mental perception. Thus, mental perception arises with the help of sense perception and grasps the object, which immediately succeeds the object of sense-perception.[3] In this sense, the Buddhists distinguish between two knowledges, sense perception and mental perception. They argue that mental perception is required in order to relate sense perception

1. *tatastebhyo vitathārthebhyo vikalpebhyaḥ tattvavyavasthānaṁ tattvena pramāṇatvena vyavasthānaṁ nirṇayaḥ*, *Ibid*, p. 523.

2. The inference as, *pratyakṣaṁ nirvikalpam arthasāmarthyāt utpatte uttarārthakṣaṇavat*, and *na santi pratyakṣe kalpanāḥ, upalabdhikṣaṇaprāptānāṁ anupalabdhikṣaṇaprāptānāmanupalambhāt, bhūtale ghaṭavat*. *Ibid*, p. 524.

3. *svaviṣayāntaraviṣayasahakāriṇendriyajñānena samantarapratyayena janitaṁ tanmanovijñānam*, *Nyāyabindu*, p. 13.

(*nirvikalpa*) to conception (*savikalpa*) which is to arise out of the former, the two being entirely heterogenous. But this argument is not accepted by all the Buddhists. For example, Dharmottara says that there is no *pramāṇa* for the existence of mental perception, though he accepts it on the authority of the Buddhist tradition.[1]

Akalaṅka does not accept the Buddhist theory of mental perception. He points out that there is only one perceptual knowledge. In the judgement, 'this is blue', there is no necessity to ascribe a mental perception other than the sense percep. tion, because this judgement is possible only by sense perception. Thus, there is only one perceptual knowledge, which is conceptual and judgemental.

In the judgement, 'this is blue', we do not find two knowledges as the Buddhists hold, for the difference between the two is not apprehended.[2] Vādirāja explains that if there were mental perception, then the difference between it and sense knowledge would be perceived, either before the sense knowledge, or simultaneously with it, or after the sense knowledge. It cannot be apprehended before the sense knowledge, because at that time the mental perception, being an effect of the sense knowledge, cannot arise before the cause. Nor can the difference be apprehended simultaneously, for the cause and the effect cannot arise together, and also because we do not experience the two perceptions simultaneously. Nor is it apprehended after the sense knowledge, for then the sense knowledge does not exist any more, and it cannot be perceived in the mental perception.

The Buddhists may reply that sense knowledge is different from mental perception in this sense that mental perception is characterised by certainty (*niścayarūpatvam*). The mental perception appears as 'this is blue', 'this is yellow' etc., but the sense perception does not have this form.

To this, Vādirāja replies that we may ascribe the same certainty to sense knowledge.[3] The Buddhists may point out that sense perception cannot have certainty because there

1. *etac ca siddhāntaprasiddhaṁ mānasaṁ pratyakṣam, na tvasya prasādhakamasti pramāṇam. Nyāyabindu*, p. 14.
2. *bhedastatra na lakṣyate. NVV*, p.525.
3. *evam aindriyajñānasyaiva niścayarūpatve ko doṣaḥ ? Ibid.*

is doubt about it. Vādirāja replies that there is also doubt about mental perception and then there is no difference between the two cases.

The Buddhists may hold that the two (the sense knowledge and the mental perception) arise at one and the same moment, possessing two different characters. And yet they are apprehended as one and the difference between them is not apprehended. The Jainas would then ask, which knowledge makes the judgement of the identity between them? The judgment is not due to sense knowledge, because sense knowledge, being *nirvikalpaka*, is not judgmental in nature. A knowledge which is not judgmental cannot make a judgment. The Buddhists may reply that the sense of identity between sense knowledge and mental perception is not a conceptual knowledge of identity but a simple *nirvikalpaka* apprehension of it. But this would lead the Buddhists to further difficulties. If this knowledge of identity is true, then there is identity and not difference between sense knowledge and mental perception. If this knowledge is false, then it cannot be *nirvikalpaka* perception, for all *nirvikalpaka*, according to the Buddhists, is true. Thus, both alternatives lead the Buddhists to unconvincing conclusions.

The mental perception also cannot be the source of the judgment of identity, because it also is non-judgmental in its nature (*tasyāpi svarūpe adhyavasāyaśūnyatvāt*).

According to the Buddhist Śāntabhadra, although the difference between the sense knowledge and mental perception is not directly perceived, yet their effects are different. The knowledge, 'this is blue', is conceptual or *savikalpaka* and cannot be caused by sense knowledge directly. Sense knowledge is *nirvikalpaka*, therefore it ('this is blue') must be caused by mental perception. For the Buddhists, concept or *vikalpa* is not possible without mental perception. But in reply Vādirāja points out that mental perception cannot be the cause of *vikalpa*, because *vikalpa* (according to the Jainas) accompanies all sense perception and so also mental perception.[1]

1. *na hi mānasaṁ vikalpasyopādānamupapannam, indriyajñānasamabhāvinastasya tataḥ prāgeva bhāvāt, tasya cendriyajñānakāryatayā paścādevotpatteḥ*, *NVV*, p. 527.

The Buddhist theory that the *vikalpa* is caused by mental perception is contradicted, according to Akalaṅka, by perception and inference. For perception shows that *vikalpa* arises from sense perception. We have the awareness, "I am experiencing colour etc., simultaneously with my eyes etc," (*mayā yugapad cakṣurādinā rūpādikam anvabhāvi*). This awareness shows that *vikalpa* arises from sense perception and not from mental perception. Further, both agreement in *presence* and agreement in *absence* show that it is the sense organ and not mental perception which causes *vikalpa*.

Dharmottara admits that the hypothesis of mental perception cannot be proved. But he accepts it because it is supported by the *Āgamas*.

Akalaṅka has another objection against the Buddhist theory of mental perception. If each sense perception has its own mental perception then it would be impossible to have a recollection of the form, "I am experiencing the colour, the taste and the smell of this fruit." On the other hand, if one mental perception may arise out of all these different sense knowledges, then why not hold, that one sense knowledge may have all these different objects? The recollection, "I am experiencing colour, taste, smell etc.," arises at once, but the mental perception of the respective sense perceptions can only arise one after another. Therefore, these mental perceptions cannot account for that recollection.[1]

5. *The Buddhist Theory of Sva-Saṁvedana*

According to the Buddhists, every consciousness and every mental phenomenon is self-conscious or *sva-saṁvedana*.[2] Akalaṅka agrees with this view because he also accepts that all knowledge is self-revealing. But he does not agree with the Buddhists that all self-cognitions are *pramāṇa* or valid knowledge. Akalaṅka holds that only determinate self-cognitions may be called valid knowledge or *pramāṇa*. He points out that if all self-consciousness were valid knowledge, then even in the state of deep sleep and a state of swoon one may be said to be perceiving, because even then, there is the awareness of the self

1. *athaikaṁ sarvaviṣayamastu kiṁ vākṣabuddhibhiḥ. NVV,* I.163.
2. *sarvacittacaittānām ātmasaṁvedanam. Nyāyabindu.* p. 14.

and this type of knowledge should also be called valid knowledge.[1]

Prajñākaragupta holds that in these states there is no knowledge and so no self-consciousness (*tadavasthasya jñānameva nāsti*). Akalaṅka argues that if there is complete absence of knowledge in these states, then this would mean a complete non-existence of the *bhāvanā* of the four noble truths in meditations.[2] In other words, if a person after meditating on the noble truths, enjoys a state of dreamless sleep, then all the effects of his meditations would be lost, and he has to begin it all anew after he wakes up.

6. *Hemacandra's Criticism*

The Buddhists define perception as *kalpanāpoḍham* (free from *kalpanā* or concept). Perception, therefore, is *nirvikalpaka* (without concept) and *abhrānta* (unerring).[3] Hemacandra points out in this connection that the above definition is untenable, for it is not relevant for practical use (*vyavahāra*). The philosophers undertake an examination of the nature of *pramāṇa*, because it is through *pramāṇa* that one determines the nature of the object and thereby becomes successful in his perceptual behaviour. If a *pramāṇa* is unsuited for practical use (*vyavahāra*), then its examination is as fruitless as counting the number of teeth of a crow. If the Buddhists reply that the *savikalpa*, which comes after *nirvikalpa*, is the cause of the activity then Hemacandra suggests that in that case the *savikalpa* should be *pramāṇa* and not the *nirvikalpa*.[4]

7. *Nyāya Definition of Pratyakṣa and Its Criticism*

(a) *Akalaṅka's View*: The *Naiyāyikas* define perception thus: *indriyārthasannikarṣotpannaṁ jñānamavyapadeśyam avyabhicāri vyavasāyātmakaṁ pratyakṣam*". The knowledge which arises out of the contact of the sense organs with the object is *pratyakṣa*. They also use the adjectives *avyapadeśya*, *avyabhicāri* and *vyavasāyātmaka*.

1. *adhyakṣa.n ātmavit sarvajñānānām abhidhīyate| svāpamūrcchādy avastho'pi pratyakṣī nāma kiṁ bhavet||* *NVV*. I. 166.
2. *vicchede hi catuḥsatyabhāvānādirvirudhyate*, *ibid*, I.167.
3. *pratyakṣaṁ kalpanāpoḍham abhrāntam*, *Nyāyabindu*, p. 8.
4. *PM* p. 23.

The word *avyapadeśya* means, *aśabdajñeya*, i.e., what is not caused by language, or the *nirvikalpa* perception. The word *avyabhicāri* is used in the sense of true knowledge which is free from error. In other words, this word excludes 'error'. And the word *vyavasāyātmaka* excludes doubt.

Akalaṅka does not accept this definition.[1] At first he says that the word *vyavasāyātmaka* does not serve to exclude anything, and so is useless. The Naiyāyikas may reply that it excludes doubt. The Jainas reply that this is not so, for doubt is already excluded by the words "sense-object-contact" (*indriyārthasannikarṣa*). The *Naiyāyikas* may still argue that doubt also is caused by sense-object-contact and so is not excluded. But the Jainas reject this view, for if doubt is caused by sense-object-contact, then with what is the sense-organ in contact in the doubt of a man in a tree ? With the tree, or the man or both ? Contact is not possible with both a tree and a man because only one is present; if there is contact with both, then there would be no doubt, and the knowledge would be valid. Doubt is not possible if the thing is present. Again, if the thing is not present, then the necessity of contact is useless. Thus doubt is not produced by sense-object-contact. In the same way, the sense-object-contact is useless in error also. In the knowledge of a snake in a rope, with what is the sense organ in contact ? The contact is not possible with a snake for the snake is not there. The contact with the rope cannot produce the knowledge of a snake because contact cannot change the form of one thing into another. Thus the word *avyabhicāri* is useless, for the word contact serves to exclude error.

The word *avyapadeśya* is also useless, because, according to the *Nyāya* theory, the judgment, "this is blue", should be said to arise not from sense-object-contact but from *nirvikalpaka* perception of the blue together with the *śabadajñāna*. Therefore, the mere word *sannikarṣa* excludes all *vyapadeśyajñāna* and the word *avyapadeśya* is useless.

The *Naiyāyikas* may suggest that perception is definable simply as the knowledge which arises from sense-object-contact. In that case, the Jainas would argue that the contact between

1. *NVV*, p. 525-40.

the self and the mind is impossible and even if it were possible it would be eternal for the self is all-pervading.

The Jainas further point out that there is no *pramāṇa* to prove that there is contact between the senses and the object. The Naiyāyikas may suggest the following proof: When the object is at a great distance or is far away, there is no sense contact with it, and there is no perception of it. If sense-object-contact were not necessary for perception, then we could perceive very distant objects, but we cannot do so. Therefore, sense-object-contact is necessary for perception.

As against the above argument, the Jainas would ask, what is this *sannikarṣa* or contact? The *Naiyāyikas* may give us a list of the six *sannikarṣas*. But they fail to give us any common property characterising all cases of *sannikarṣa*. Thus, they are not able to tell us what precisely is *sannikarṣa*.

The word *Jñāna* in the definition is useless for the expression *indriyārthasannikarṣotpannam* can only mean a knowledge and nothing else. The *Naiyāyikas* may reply that pleasure and pain also arise from sense-object-contact and the word *jñāna* is used to exclude them. The Jainas reject this and hold that pleasure and pain are also forms of knowledge because they also are self-revealing.

Therefore, the *Nyāya* definition is too narrow. It does not apply to perception of pleasure and pain, where there is no sense-object-contact.

(*b*) *Prabhācandra's View* : Prabhācandra in his *Prameyakamalamārtaṇḍa* also rejects the definition.[1] He points out, in the first place, that this definition is too narrow for it does not apply to non-sensuous perception (*atīndriyapratyakṣa*). Further, if perception arises out of the sense-object-contact then there would be no omniscience.

Secondly, this definition does not apply to perception of pleasure and pain, etc. There is no contact between the sense organs and pleasure and pain etc. But pleasure and pain etc. are knowledge and they are self-revealing.

(*c*) *Hemacandra's View* : Hemacandra, while examining the above *Nyāya* definition points out that the *Naiyāyikas* like Trilocana and Vācaspati go against the interpretations given by

1. *PKM*, p. 220.

the old masters and interpret the definition as follows. The definition of perception is merely that perception is the knowledge which arises from the contact of the sense organs with the object and which is unerring. By introducing the word *yataḥ* they point out that *pratyakṣa pramāṇa* or the source of perceptual knowledge is that from which such knowledge arises. It may be either of the nature of knowledge or of the nature of non-knowledge. The resulting knowledge is of two kinds : *avikalpakam* or indeterminate and *savikalpakam* or determinate. The part of the definition *avyapadeśyaṁ vyavasāyātmakam* is really a classification of perception. Indeterminate perception is *avyapadeśyam* and determinate perception is *vyavasāyātmakam*.

Hemacandra considers this interpretation, untenable,[1] as it does not recognise the *prāmāṇya* of the two kinds of perceptual knowledge but instead supports the *prāmāṇya* of the sense-object-contact, which is not a knowledge, and for this purpose introduces the word *yataḥ* into the original definition. How can sense-object-contact etc., which are of the nature of *ajñāna* or non-knowledge, become the extraordinary cause of the manifestation of the object ? For it is not necessary that the former are always followed by the latter. Even if there is sense-object-contact, there may not be manifestation of the object, only if there is knowledge there is manifestation of object. Knowledge is, therefore, the extraordinary cause, for it is immediately followed by the effect.

Hemacandra next asks, what is meant by *sannikarṣa* ? If it means relations like *saṁyoga* or conjunction and is different from mere *yogyatā*, then they cannot be *sannikarṣa* between the eye and its object because the eye is *aprāpyakārī*. The eye apprehends the object, even if it is mediated by a piece of glass or by some other transparent substance. It cannot be said that the eye, since it is an instrumental cause like an axe, is *prāpyakārī* for such an inference will be contradicted by the instance of a magnet which attracts from a distance.[2]

1. *PM*, p. 22.

2. The Jaina theory that the eye and *manas* are *aprāpyakārī* will be explained in Ch. IV.

8. *The Sāṁkhya Definition of Perception*

According to the *Sāṁkhyas*, *pratyakṣa* is the modification of the sense organs into the form of the object perceived. The sense organs go out and assume the form of the object perceived. Akalaṅka rejects this definition because, as he points out, on this view even error would be true perception. For, when one sees two moons by mistake his visual sense organ assumes the form of two moons and so the perception must be true. But this is absurd.[1]

The old *Sāṁkhya* defines perception as the indeterminate knowledge residing in ears, etc. As against this definition, Hemacandra argues that since the ear, etc. are non-conscious, the knowledge residing in them would also be non-conscious, and so how can it be *pramāṇa* ? If it be said that it becomes conscious through contact with consciousness, then it is better to say that consciousness alone is *pramāṇa*. Further, an indeterminate knowledge cannot be *pramāṇa* as stated earlier.[2]

Īśvara Kṛṣṇa has defined perception as judgment about each object.[3] This definition is also applied to inference. If *prati* means that the object should be before one self, then even in inference it may be so, as when we infer 'this hill has fire'. If it be said that perception is that judgment about an object before me which is not inference, then Hemacandra replies that such a definition requires that we should first give a definition of inference.

9. *The Mīmāṁsakas' Definition of Pratyakṣa*

The *Mīmāṁsakas* want to show that perception does not give us knowledge of *dharma* and so define perception as the knowledge or *buddhi* which arises in the self through the contact of the sense-organs with something that is present. This perception is not a cause of knowledge of *dharma*, because it can only know something which is present.

According to Hemacandra, this definition is too wide

1. *śrotrādivṛttiḥ pratyakṣaṁ yadi taimirikādiṣu prasaṅgaḥ kiṁtadvṛttis-tadvikārānukāriṇī*, *NVV*, I.168.

2. *PM*, I.I.8.

3. *prativiṣayeṣu śrotrādīnāṁ śabdādiviṣayeṣu adhyavasāyo dṛṣṭaṁ, pratyakṣa-mityarthaḥ*, *SK*, 5.

because doubt and error also arise in the self through contact with the senses. If it be said that in perception the contact should be with a real object, then Hemacandra replies that though the definition does not apply to hallucination which has no object, it does apply to error and doubt which have real objects. To this the *Mīmāṁsakas* may reply that we can exclude doubt and error with the help of the word *samprayoga* for the word *sam* means *samyak* or right contact. This excludes *duṣprayoga* or defective contact which takes place in the case of error and doubt. Hemacandra replies that the rightness of the contact is supersensible and so is not known by perception; and so can be known only through its effect, that is, the knowledge. But the knowledge is not known directly as having been caused by right contact. Therefore, the rightness of the contact cannot be apprehended.[1]

It is not enough to say that in the case of perception there is contact of the senses with the very object which is known. If there is contact with another object then it is not perception, but Hemacandra points out that even this definition would apply to doubt. Even in the case of doubt also there is contact of the sense with the object of knowledge although a doubt has two objects (Is this a man or a tree ?). Yet with one of these two the senses are in contact. Further, the definition also is too narrow, for there is no contact of the eye with its object in the case of visual perception. The eye, as stated earlier is *aprāpyakārī.*

1. *PM*, p. 23.

PART TWO
EMPIRICAL PERCEPTION

CHAPTER IV

EMPIRICAL PERCEPTION

1. *The Jaina Definitions*

In the Jaina *Āgamas*, empirical perception is called *ābhinibodhika-jñāna* and *matijñāna*. Later on, when the Jaina logic developed, the term *indriya-pratyakṣa* or *sāṁvyavahārika pratyakṣa* came to be used in the sense of empirical perception. Though the words are different yet they are used synonymously for empirical perception which is caused by five sense organs and/or mind. The *Sāṁvyavahārika* is that type of perception which arises with the help of the sense organs and mind.

Akalaṅka defines empirical knowledge thus : A knowledge of the object caused by sense organs, and which is able to avoid undesirable and attain to desirable and which is limited, such knowledge is called empirical knowledge.[1]

Māṇikyanandi defines empirical perception as the knowledge which is caused by sense organs and mind, which is limited and which is *sāṁvyavahārika*.[2] Prabhācandra explains *sāṁvyavahārika* to mean which enables one to avoid the undesirable and attain the desirable.

Hemacandra defines empirical perception thus,[3] it arises with the help of the sense organs and the mind. The sense organs and the mind are the instrumental cause of this knowledge. Therefore, the sense organs and the mind have their own place in this definition of the *sāṁvyavahārika pratyakṣa*. The word *ātmā* in the definition is used in the sense of its nature. The nature of this knowledge is analysed in terms of its stages. It has four stages—*avagraha*, *īhā*, *avāya* and *dhāraṇā*. These stages which arise one after another are not totally different. The preceding stage becomes the succeeding one.

1. *hitāhitāptinirmuktikṣamam indriyanirmitaṁ, yaddeśato'rthajñānaṁ tad indriyādhyakṣam ucayate*, *NVV*, p. 105.

2. *indriyānīndriyanimittaṁ deśataḥ sāṁvyavahārikam*, *PKM*, p. 229.

3. *indriyamanonimitto avagrahehāvāyadhāraṇātmā sāṁvyavahārikam*, *PM*, I.1.20.

The word *saṁvyavahāra* means right action, either of the nature of *pravṛtti* (positive) or *nivṛtti* (negative). The knowledge which is the cause of such *vyavahāra* or action is *sāṁvyavahārika pratyakṣa*.

2. *INDRIYAS* (*Sense Organs*)

In the definition of *sāṁvyavaharika pratyakṣa* what is meant by *indriya*? The word *indriya* may be derived in various ways. Hemacandra suggests several meanings.[1] It may mean that which is the mark of the self or *Indra*. The sense organs are the instrumental causes of the act of perception, but where there is an instrument there must be a person who makes use of it. Therefore, from the activity of sense organs we may infer the existence of the self. The word *indriya* may also mean that which helps the self to apprehend objects. Though the self is omniscient, yet it cannot know the objects by itself when it is under the influence of a *karmic* matter (ignorance). It is the sense organs and mind which make it possible for the self to know objects. Thus the senses and mind are the instruments by which the self can get experiences.

Most systems of Indian philosophy have distinguished between the outer structure of a sense organ and the sense organ itself. The ear and the eye-ball which we see are not the real auditory and visual sense organs respectively. They are only the external supports or *adhiṣṭhāna* of the sense organs. The sense organs themselves, on the other hand, are held to be super-sensible, though they are generally taken to be physical. The Jainas also distinguish between the physical sense organs and psychical sense organs. What is now in this distinction is that the primary sense organ, according to them, is not at all physical; it is of the nature of consciousness.

The *Sāṁvyavahārika-pratyakṣa* is of five types, based on the nature and function of five sense organs. Each of them is structurally of two parts, the physical and the psychical.[2] The physical part is called *dravyendriya* and the psychical part

1. *Ibid*, I.1.21.

2. *sparśarasagandharūpaśabdagrahaṇalakṣaṇāni sparśarasanaghrāṇacakṣuḥśrotrāṇi indriyāṇi dravyabhāvabhedāni*, *PM*, I.1.21.

is called *bhāvendriya*. Here the word *dravyendriya* defines the generic qualities of the sense organs, which have particular forms, either external or internal; the external form aspect is called *nirvṛtti* and the internal is called *upakaraṇa*.[1] The external and internal shapes are made of *pudgala* or matter. The word *dravya* is also used in the sense of what is secondary. The *dravyendriya* then means secondary sense organs, because they are nonconscious and in the process of experience they do not produce knowledge without the help of the *bhāvendriya* or psychical sense organs, which are consciousness. It may be called the sense of faculty.

The psychical part of a sense organ or the *bhāvendriya* defines two special qualities of that organ. The word *bhāva* is used as having the special meaning of importance or primacy. *Bhāvendriya* then means what possesses the property of *indriyatva* directly and not derivatively.

The Jainas hold that the material cause of the physical sense organs is a particular kind of *pudgala*, i.e., a particular kind of physical substance (*jaḍa-dravyaviśeṣa*),[2] while the psychical sense organs are of the nature of consciousness. They have two capacities which are called *labdhi* and *Upayoga*.[3] *Labdhi* is the power of the sense organ due to which the object is apprehended.[4] If there is no *labdhi* a sense organ cannot apprehend its object. And *upayoga* is the activity of consciousness towards the object.[5] If there is no activity towards the object, the object cannot be apprehended. Thus *labdhi* and *upayoga* are the special properties of the psychical sense organs. Without the psychical element, the senses would remain material in their nature and would not be able to produce knowledge. In this way the Jainas escape from the difficulty arising from a materialistic account of the sense organs.[6]

1. *nirvṛtti upakaraṇe dravyendriyam*, *TS*, II. 17.
2. *dravyendriyaṁ niyatākāraḥ pudgalaḥ*, *PM*, I.1.22.
3. *bhāvendriyaṁ labdhyupayogaḥ*, *PM*, I.1.23.
4. *arthagrahaṇaśaktir labdhiḥ*, *NKC*, p. 115
5. *ubhayo yaḥ punaḥ arthagrahaṇavyāpāraḥ*, *Ibid.*
6. *PKM*, p. 229.

3. *The Nyāya View of Sense Organs*[1]

The *Nyāya-Vaiśeṣikas* hold that the five *bhūtas*—earth, water, light, sky and air—are the material causes of the five sense organs; the five *bhūtas* are all physical substances. Each sense organ is constituted by a particular *bhūta*, and therefore, is able to apprehend the specific quality belonging to it. The olfactory sense (*ghrāṇa*) is the organ of apprehending smell, and it is constituted by earth, to which smell originally belongs as an attribute. The gustatory sense (*rasanā*) is the condition of taste sensation, and it is constituted by water. The visual sense (*cakṣu*) is the cause of colour sensation and it is constituted by the element light (*tejas*), the element of light is not manifested by touch. The cutaneous sense (*tvak*) is the sense of touch sensation; it is constituted by the element air, for like the air it manifests the quality of touch. The auditory sense (*śrotra*) is the means of sensation of sound; it is constituted by the element *ākāśa*; because the quality of sound belongs to *ākāśa*.

According to the *Naiyāyikas*, a particular sense organ is constituted by a particular element because the sense organ can apprehend only that quality of the object by which it is constituted. The Jainas reject this view. They hold that any one particular element (*bhūta*) is not the material cause of a sense organ. And it is not true that a particular sense organ apprehends only that quality by which it is constituted. According to the Jainas, the physical sense organs are made of by the *pudgalas* (matters) and each *pudgala* contains *rūpa*, *rasa*, *gandha* and *sparśa*; therefore it is not necessary that a particular sense organ should be made of a particular quality which belongs to it.

According to the *Naiyāyikas*, the organ of smell is constituted by the element earth because it apprehends smell, the quality of the earth (*pṛthvi*).

The Jainas point out that this is not true. The inference is vitiated by the fallacy of *anaikāntika-hetu*, because in some cases smell is manifested not by earth but by sun rays or also by rain water, but sun rays or water are not made of earth. The *Nyāya* view is that the organ of taste is the quality of water. The Jainas reject this because in some cases salt acts as an agent

1. *NKC*, p. 156.

which manifests taste, but salt is not made of water. Therefore, all that manifests taste is not made of water. Thus, the organ of taste is not constituted only by water. In the same way, the eyes cannot be said to be constituted by only the element of light just because the eyes manifest colour. A jewel or a magnifying glass may manifest colour though it is not made of light. The sense of touch is not constituted by air for it is found that camphor placed in a jar of water manifests cold touch but the camphor is not an airy substance. As regards the sense of hearing, the Jainas point out that the *Nyāya* theory is based on the *Nyāya* doctrine that sound is a quality of *ākāśa*. The Jainas do not accept this latter doctrine.

4. *The Sāṁkhya View of Sense Organs*

According to the *Sāṁkhyas*, the material cause of sense organ is *ahaṅkāra* which is a kind of subtle substance born of *prakṛti*. The Jainas do not accept this view; they hold that *ahaṅkāra* is not the material cause of the sense organs but they are made by *pudgala* (matter). Therefore, the sense organs are not *āhaṅkārika*. The Jainas reject the *Sāṁkhya* view of sense organs by advancing the following arguments:—

(i) The Jainas hold that the sense organs are not *āhaṅkārika*, because they are non-conscious and also instruments; a non-conscious instrument cannot be *āhaṅkārika*, just as an axe; therefore, the sense organs are not *āhaṅkārika*.[1] (ii) Again they argue that the sense organs are not *āhaṅkārika*, because they are sense organs, as in the case of the motor organs; though mind is a sense organ, yet the physical mind is not *āhaṅkārika* according to the Jainas : and the psychical mind is not an exception to the above rule for it is conscious and not a non-conscious instrument. (iii) Again the senses are not *āhaṅkārika*, because they are the causes of definite kinds of knowledge and judgment. What is the cause of a definite kind of knowledge and judgment cannot be *āhaṅkārika*, just as a colour which is a cause of the manifestation of colour. These are not *āhaṅkārika* because each of them manifests a particular object and what manifests a particular object, cannot be *āhaṅkārika*, just

1. *nāhaṅkāriṇi indriyāṇi, acetanatve sati karaṇatvād vāsyādivat*, *NKC*, p. 157.

as a lamp. Therefore, the sense organs are not *āhaṅkārika*. (iv) Further, the sense organs are not *āhaṅkārika* because they are the locus (*āśraya*) of the action of purification by something material, as in the case of a mirror. What is the locus of such action cannot be *āhaṅkārika*, just as a mirror.[1] A mirror may be cleaned by rubbing, an eye is purified by applying ointments. Therefore, the sense organs are not *āhaṅkārika* but *paudgalika*. The mind is also not *āhaṅkārika* because the mind is not limited to manifest a particular object. What is not so limited is not *āhaṅkārika*, just as the self.[2] Therefore, by the above arguments it is proved that the physical sense organs are not *āhaṅkārika* but they are *paudgalika* or made by *pudgala* (matter).

5. *Function of the Senses*

The function of the senses is to produce perception of objects. But how do the sense organs function to give us perception of objects? Do they produce perception by their direct contact with the object, or do they give us perception of objects without any contact with them? In other words, are the sense organs *prāpayakārī* or *aprāpyakārī*? There are different views regarding the function of different sense organs.

According to the Buddhists, all sense organs are *aprāpyakārī* (they function without direct contact with their objects). According to the *Nyāya*, *Sāṁkhya*, *Mimāṁsā* and *Vedānta* systems, all sense organs are *prāpyakārī*, (the sense organs produce perception by their direct contact with their objects). But, the Jainas hold that amongst the five sense organs only the eye is *aprāpyakārī* and the other four sense organs are *prāpyakārī*. The senses of touch, taste, smell and hearing produce perception by direct contact with their objects. But the eye does not perceive its object by direct contact.

6. *The Nyāya View of Prāpyakāritva of Eye*

According to the *Naiyāyikas*, the eye is *prāpyakārī*, i.e.,

1. *nāhaṅkārīṇi indriyāṇi paudgalikā'nugrahopaghātāśrayatvāt darpaṇādivat*, *NKC*, p. 158.

2. *mano'pi nāhaṅkārikam aniyataviṣayatvād ātmavaditi*, *NKC*, p. 158

the eye apprehends an object only if it is in contact with it. They prove it with the help of the following inference. The eye is *prāpykārī* because it is an outer sense organ (*bāhyendriya*), just as the organ of touch. The Jainas reject this inference. Thus, Prabhācandra asks,[1] as to what is meant in this inference by *bāhyendriyatva*. Does it mean 'being directed towards an outer object', or does it mean 'being in an external place?' In the first case, there would be *anaikāntika* fallacy because the mind also is directed towards the outer objects and so possesses the *hetu* but it is not *prāpyakārī*. In the second case, the *hetu* would be *asiddha* (being absent in the *pakṣa*) because, according to the *Naiyāyikas*, the eye is a form of light, and the locus of the light is the eye-ball and not a place outside. And so in this sense, the eye would not be an outer sense organ.

Again, does the eye mean the eye-ball or the rays of light which emanate from the eyeball. If the eye means the eye-ball, then the inference would be contradicted by perception, because we do not experience that the eye balls leave the body and come in contact with the outer objects. If the eye means the rays of light, then the *dharmī* would be *asiddha* because the rays of light are not perceived. If they were perceived, there would have been no controversy about whether the eye is the eye ball or the rays of light. If the eye means a luminous substance (*tejodravya*) which goes out from the eye-balls in the form of rays and then manifests the object, then it cannot be explained why one should keep one's eye open in order to be able to see, and also why applications of the *añjana* should improve one's vision. Only if the rays cannot go out of the eye-balls, it is necessary to keep the eye open in order to see. If the eye is not the eye-ball then the application of the *añjana* to the eye ball would not possibly improve the vision.

If the rays of light went out of the eye-balls and came into contact with the object perceived, then we should be able to see those luminous rays since they possess shining colour and also warm touch. But we do not perceive any such substance, therefore the eye does not comprise such substance. Human eyes are perceived without such shining rays. The *Naiyāyikas*

1. For the following arguments see *PKM*, p. 220.

prove that the eye is luminous on the ground that it manifests only colour (*rūpa*) even if there are things other than colour (*rūpa*), as in the case of a lamp. A lamp manifests only colour and it is also a luminous substance. Whatever manifests only colour, even if other things are present, must be a luminous substance.

This inference is contradicted by perception, because the eye is perceived to be without shining colour and warm touch; therefore, it cannot be luminous. It is also contradicted by the following inference: the eye is not luminous, because it manifests darkness. Whatever is luminous does not manifest darkness, as in the case of light (which is luminous and does not manifest darkness).

Further, if the eyes were luminous, then they would not require the help of light for perceiving. A lamp does not need another lamp to do its job.

If it be objected that if the eye is not related to its object how can knowledge arise in it, the Jainas reply that knowledge does not arise in the eyes, it arises only in the self.

It may be asked, if the eyes are *aprāpyakārī*, then why are they unable to see everything? To this the reply is that every sense-organ has its own power and capacity. The principle is, a thing can do something only if it has the *yogyatā* to do it. Even the *Naiyāyikas* have to accept the principle of *yogyatā*. According to the *Nyāya* theory, the cause and the effect are completely different and so there is no reason why a particular cause should produce only a particular effect and not all possible effects. They can only avoid this difficulty by the idea of *yogyatā*.

The Jainas may make use of the following inference to prove that the eyes are *aprāpyakārī*. The eyes are *aprāpyakārī* because they do not manifest what is too close to them (for example, the *añjana* in the eye ball is not seen). Whatever is *prāpyakārī* manifests what is too close, as for example the ear; the ear can hear sounds produced by a mosquito within the ear hole.

It may be objected that the organ of touch, which is the skin, is *prāpyakārī* but does not apprehend things too close to it inside the body. To this it may be replied that what happens inside the body is the cause of apprehension and not its object. That the eyes are *aprāpyakārī* may again be proved in the following way. "The eyes do not go out and come in contact with their objects, for they possess *indriyatva*, as in the case of the organ of touch."

7. *The Buddhist View of Aprāpyakāritva of Ear*

The Buddhists believe that the sense organ of hearing is *aprāpyakārī*, for if it were *prāpyakārī* then there could not be judgment about the nearness or distance of the sounds which we hear. Whatever apprehends an objects as being far or near must be *aprāpyakārī*; the eye, for example, apprehends a tree as being far or near and the eye is not *prāpyakārī*. By this kind of inference the Buddhists try to prove that the organ of hearing is *aprāpyakārī*. If it be objected against this that there cannot be in that case the impact of sound on one's ear, the Buddhists reply that very bright light may dazzle one's eyes even though the eyes are not in contact with it. The cause of impact in case of light is brilliance, and in the case of sound its loudness.

Against the above inference, Prabhācandra raises the following objections.[1] The inference is contradicted by perception, for when there is the noise of a mosquito with in the ear we hear it and this would contact with the organ of hearing. Therefore, it cannot be said that the ears apprehend their object without coming into contact with them.

Secondly, the *hetu* i.e., *dūrādipratyayagrāhyatva* is *anaikāntika* for, the organ of smell apprehends its objects by coming into contact with it and yet it does apprehend its objects as being far or near. We, for example, say that the smell of the lotus comes from far away while the smell of jasmine is very close by. Is sound by its very nature far away, or is it caused by something which is far away, or does this sound come from a place far away, or does sound remain in that place far away ?

Not the first, because in that case a sound may be by its very nature near and would be apprehended as such.

Not the second, for smell is also caused by something which is far away and yet the organ of smell is *prāpyakārī*.

1. For the following arguments, see *NKC*, p. 83.

Not the third, for the same also holds good of smell which comes in contact with the organ of smell.

Not the last one, because if the sound remained in the place far away then one has to explain why one hears the sound when there is a favourable wind and does not hear it when the wind is unfavourable. One can only explain this if one assumes that the sound travels from the place of its origin to the ear, but in that case the sense of hearing would be *prāpyakārī*.

Further, if the sound which is heard remained in its own place of origin, then the loud sound of the trumpet and the faint hum of a mosquito would both be heard together and the former could not overpower the latter.

8. *The Relation Amongst the Sense Organs*

The Jainas accept the relation of difference and identity (*bhedābheda*) amongst the sense-organs themselves, while the other systems hold either only difference or only identity. According to the Jainas, the sense-organs are different in one respect and identical in another respect. They are different in respect of their qualities (*paryāya*) and identical in respect of the substance (*dravya*). All the sense-organs are non-different because they are made of the same substance and they are all material. But they are different regarding their qualities; each sense organ has its own special quality. In this sense, they are different.[1]

Hemacandra argues thus : if there is only non-difference (*abheda*) amongst the senses then there would be no difference between the experiences of two sense-organs. By the sense of touch one can have the experience of taste. And also there would be no idea of different sense-organs. If one sense-organ is good or defective, then all the others would be so. Different sense-organs produce different experiences. If there is no difference amongst them, then there would be no difference in these experiences.

Again, if only there is difference (*bheda*) amongst the senses, then it would be impossible for them all to produce together one knowledge as in the case of a sense-organ belonging to a different series.

1. *teṣāṁ ca parasparaṁ syādbhedo dravyārthadeśāt, syādabhedaḥ paryāyārthadeśāt*, *PM*, p. 17.

Those who maintain that there is only difference (*bheda*) among the five sense-organs say that the sense-organs are different but it is the mind which produces knowledge and, therefore, there is no harm to accept only difference amongst them. Hemacandra, however, points out that the mind cannot do this, for the mind is independent of the sense organs.[1]

In the same way, it can be shown that the sense-organs are neither wholly different nor wholly non-different from the self. If the sense-organs were merely identical with the self then they would be subjects of knowledge, or the self would be an instrument, or both would possess both the characters. On the other hand, if they are wholly different from the self then the self would not at all be an instrument, like an instrument belonging to another series. Therefore, *anekāntavāda* has to be accepted.

9. *The Jaina Theory of Mind*

According to the Jainas, mind has an important place in empirical knowledge. Not only the senses but also mind is the instrumental cause of empirical knowledge.

In the *Tattvārtha Sūtra*, mind is defined as *anindriya*, which means *antaḥkaraṇa* or the internal sense.[2] It is different from the external sense organs. The objects of sense perception are also objects of mind. Mind is also a sense of internal perceptions like pleasure, pain etc. Also it is the means of scriptural knowledge.[3] Thus mind is defined as internal sense.

Hemacandra in his *Pramāṇa-Mīmāṁsā* defines mind as the instrument of the self which apprehends everything.[4] Mind can acquire knowledge of all objects, in the sense that it is not subject to the limitations which we find in the case of the five sense organs. Each sense organ can apprehend only a particular kind of object. For example, the sense of touch cannot apprehend smell. But the mind has no such limitations. Mind can grasp anything which comes into contact with the five sense-organs. Mind is defined as *karaṇa* or the instrument of the

1. *na tasya indriyanirapekṣasya tajjanakatvābhāvāt*, *PM*, p. 17.
2. *TS*, I.14.
3. *Ibid*, II.22.
4. *sarvārthagrahaṇaṁ manaḥ*, *PM*, I.1.34.

self. If the mind were defined as what apprehends everything, then this definition would apply also to the self which is omniscient. Therefore, the mind is defined as the *instrument* for knowing all objects. The self is not an instrument but the mind is.[1] Though empirical knowledge is based on mind and the sense organs, yet it may be divided into two forms, the *indriyaja* and the *manonimitta*—that which arises mainly from the senses and that which is mainly due to mind, which we may also call external perception and internal perception. Mind is *aprāpyakārī* according to the Jainas, because there is no direct contact between the object and the mind. They do not accept the *Nyāya* view of *prāpyakāritva* of mind. They point out that if the mind were *prāpyakārī*, then it would go out of its place and meet the objects near or far, in the state of waking as well as in sleeping, but in practice, we do not find this. Therefore, mind is *aprāpyakārī*. A question may arise; is mind physical or non-physical? According to the Jainas, mind is both, physical and non-physical. In respect of its modifications mind is physical; it is called *dravyamana* because it is made of the *pudgalas* or matters which are called *vargaṇā*. But in another aspect, it is non-physical or conscious; it is called *bhāvamaṇah*. *Bhāva* is the conscious aspect of the mind. If mind were only physical, then perception would be impossible.

10. *The Nyāya Theory of Mind*[2]

According to the *Nyāya-Vaiśeṣikas*, mind is a sense organ; it is an internal sense-organ. But it is eternal and non-physical; it is not constituted by the physical elements, like earth, water etc. Mind is called an internal sense organ because the internal perception depends on mind, just as external perception depends on external senses. The internal perception of pleasure, pain, desire etc. cannot be produced by the external senses like sense of sight, hearing etc., Again, mind is also the condition for the external perception; according to the *Nyāya-Vaiśeṣikas* the external senses can perceive objects only when they are in contact with the mind.

Mind is atomic and exists in contact with the self. It comes in contact with the self and sense-organs and gives rise

1. *PM*, I. 1.24.
2. Bhattacharya, H.S., *Reals in the Jaina Metaphysics*, p. 265.

to perception. It is not extended, for at one moment it cannot be in contact with many objects. If mind were an extended organ, we could have many perceptions at one time.

The Jainas do not agree with the *Naiyāyikas'* view that mind is an eternal substance. According to the Jainas mind is both eternal and non-eternal. It is eternal in one aspect and non-eternal in another aspect. Mind is eternal only in the sense that it is constituted by *pudgalas* (matter), which are eternal. In other words, the *pudgalas* are the essence of the mind. Thus, in the aspect of *dravya*, mind is eternal; as a substance, it is eternal. On the other hand, with the aspect of its qualities or *paryāya* it is not eternal because the qualities of mind, pleasure, pain etc., are changing.

The Jainas do not accept the *Nyāya* view that mind is atomic. They point out that if mind were atomic, it could not come into contact with the self at the same time as its contact with the sense organs. Mind is, according to the Jainas, *madhyamaparimāṇī*.

11. *The Sāṁkhya Theory of Mind*[1]

According to the *Sāṁkhyas*, mind is an internal sense organ but it is a physical substance and it is unconscious, being effect of unconscious *prakṛti*. Though mind is internal sense yet it helps the external senses to produce knowledge. The function of mind is to change sensation into concept. The Jainas do not agree with the *Sāṁkhyas* that mind is unconscious. They ask, how can an unconscious entity become an instrument of conscious process? How can the unconscious mind change the sensations into concept? Therefore, they hold that mind is not unconscious; it is rather of the nature of consciousness.

12. *The Causes of Perception*

Some hold that mind and the sense-organs are not the only causes of perception, but the object and light also are the causes of perception. The Jainas point out that the object and light are not the necessary conditions of perception.[2] They argue like this : the object and light are not the causes of

1. *Bhattacharya, H.S., Reals in the Jaina Metaphysics*, p. 251.
2. *nārthālokau kāraṇaṁ paricchedyatvāt tamovat, PKM*, p. 231.

perception because they are objects of knowledge. Whatever are the objects of knowledge are not the causes of perception, just as darkness. Everybody knows that darkness is an object of knowledge but it is not the cause of perception. It is the *pratibandhaka* of knowledge; due to darkness an object may not be apprehended. If the object would be the cause of knowledge then the presence of the object must be necessary for knowledge and if it would be so, then there would be no knowledge of the objects of the past and of the future. If light were the cause of perception, then there would be no knowledge in darkness, and one would not have the knowledge of darkness itself.

The opponent may ask : what is the harm if the object and light are accepted as the causes of knowledge? The Jainas reply that if the object and light are accepted as the causes of knowledge then they would not be the objects of knowledge (*jñeya*) at the same time, just as the eye (which is a cause of perception but not its object). The *Naiyāyikas* hold that knowledge is the effect of object. They argue like this : knowledge is the effect of object and light, because there is the relation of *anvaya-vyatireka* between knowledge and object or light. What are related by this relation are cause and effect; just as fire and smoke. Smoke is related by the *anvaya-vyatireka* with fire; therefore smoke is the effect of fire. In the same way, knowledge is related to the object and light by this relation; therefore, knowledge is the effect of object and light. If there is no object or light, there would be no knowledge. The Jainas reject this argument and point out that it is not true. Knowledge is not the effect of object and light. There is no *anvayavyatireka* relation between them. In knowledge of snake in a rope there is no object of knowledge (snake) but there is knowledge. In this example, knowledge is not the effect of object, because the object itself is absent. Again, light is also not the cause of knowledge. And there is no *anvaya-vyatireka* relation between them. In some cases, there is no light but there is knowledge. For example, nocturnal animals can see in darkness. And some kind of perceptual knowledge is possible in darkness, just as knowledge of taste and knowledge of words.

The opponent may ask : if light is not the cause of knowledge then there is no necessity of a lamp. The Jainas reply that although light manifests the object yet it does not produce knowledge. Knowledge is the effect of mind and sense-organs, not of the light of a lamp, because knowledge is possible without light.[1]

Hemacandra also does not accept the object and light as the causes of perception. He says that the object and light are not the causes for producing knowledge, because there is no *vyatireka-vyāpti* between them.[2] The external objects and light are not the direct causes of experience of sight, it is not denied that they are like space and time etc., remote causes. The eye is admitted to be auxiliary, like *añjana* etc. Why are they not direct causes? Because there is absence of *vyatireka*. The cause of ascertaining a casual relation is not that when one is present the other must be present, but the fact that when the one is absent the other is absent. This latter fact is called *vyatireka*. This is not present in the case of the supposed causality of the object and light. For, there may be knowledge of water in a desert or mirage although water is really absent. The *yogīs* apprehend past and future objects and such objects cannot be causes. If they are causes then they would possess causal efficiency and so would be existent and would not be past and future.

1. *PKM*, p. 233.
2. *nārthālokau jñānasya nimittamavyatirekāt*, *PM*, I.1.25.

CHAPTER V

STAGES OF EMPIRICAL PERCEPTION

1. *Four Stages*

According to the Jainas, sense-organs and mind are the instruments, by which empirical perception is caused. The nature of this knowledge will now be analysed in terms of its stages. Empirical perception is the result of the contact of the senses and mind with the object. But it arises not only by this contact; there is also a process of perception. In this process, the Jainas distinguish between four stages, every kind of empirical perception which passes through these stages arising one after another, but are not totally different from each other.[1] The preceding stage becomes the succeeding one. These four stages are : *avagraha*, *īhā*, *avāya* and *dhāraṇā*.

Avagraha : The first stage *avagraha* refers to the most primitive stage of perception. It is the first to arise out of the contact between the sense organs and the object. Amongst the Jaina authors there are two views regarding the exact nature of *avagraha*. (i) Umāsvāti defines *avagraha* as indeterminate perception. The contact between the sense organs and the object produces the merely indeterminate perception, wherein the sense organs grasp the object without knowing any of its special qualities. For example, in darkness one has the sensation of touch, without knowing with what one is in contact; there is only a feeling of something (*yat kiṅcit*). This is called *avagraha*. In this sense, *avagraha* is indeterminate perception without any name, quality,[2] etc. It is the first stage of perception; it is indeterminate perception.

(ii) Other logicians like Pūjyapāda, Devānandi, Akalaṅka, Vidyānandi and Hemacandra define *avagraha* as determinate perception. They hold that *avagraha* is the primitive stage of perception but it arises after *darśana* or the mere sensa-

1. *krameṇotpadyamānānāmapi avagrahādīnāṁ nātyantikabhedaḥ kiṁtu pūrvapūrvasya uttarottararūpatayā pariṇāmādekātmakatvamiti*, *PM*, I.1.20.
2. *TS* (Hindi tr.), p. 24.

tion of the object. Pūjyapāda points out that it is the first apprehension after the sense-object-contact.[1] For example, after the mere sensation of something, one apprehends a cloth with its whiteness. Thus, it is not mere sensation but the determinate perception of the cloth.

The other logicians also followed this view. Akalaṅka defines *avagraha* as determinate perception, and explains it as arising due to the sense-object-contact. It is the first apprehension of the object, not merely the sensation.[2] Hemacandra points out that indeterminate perception is not *avagraha*, but *avagraha* arises due to the sense-object-contact when the *darśana* (sensation) transforms itself into the determinate perception.[3]

Thus there are two different views amongst the Jainas about the nature of *avagraha*. According to the older one, *avagraha* is mere sensation or indeterminate perception. But the second one defines *avagraha* as determinate perception, arising after mere sensation (*darśana*).

Avagraha has further been analysed into two stages : *vyañjanāvagraha* and *arthāvagraha*.[4]

Vyañjanāvagraha : It is the earlier stage. It may be called a contact awareness because in this stage there is only relation of the sense-organs with the object but there is no sensation in the subject. For example, a man in sleep receives a succession of sound of something; there is the contact of sound with his auditory sense organ, but he does not have any kind of sensation at first. But after sometime, at a particular state, he becomes conscious of that sound. So far he may not be aware of this sound although the auditory stimulation is there. This auditory stimulation is the *vyañjanāvagraha* in this case. Though there is no conscious awareness in the *vyañjanāvagraha* yet it is not an unconscious state because it is the cause of conscious awareness which arises in *arthāvagraha*.[5]

Arthāvagraha : It is the second stage of *avagraha*. It may be called the stage of conscious awareness of the object, because

1. *SS* (Eng. tr.), p. 29.
2. *viṣayaviṣayisannipātāntaramādyagrahaṇam avagrahaḥ*, *NKC*, I.5.
3. *akṣārthayoge darśanāntaram arthagrahaṇam avagrahaḥ*, *PM*, I.1.26.
4. *dvividho avagraho vyañjanasyārthasya ca*, *TB*, I.18.
5. *TS* (Hindi Tr.), pp. 35-36.

in this stage the subject has the perception of the object. In other words, as a person becomes conscious, the stage of *vyañjanāvagraha* is over and it transforms itself into *arthāvagraha*. Thus, *vyañjanāvagraha* is a necessary antecedent of *arthāvagraha*.

Īhā : After *avagraha* there comes *Īhā*. In *avagraha* there is an awareness of the object, but *īhā* is an intellectual enquiry (*mateḥ-ceṣṭā*)[1] about the nature of the object. Supposing, there may still be doubt about what the source of the sound is. Is it produced by a musical instrument or by some other means ? This doubt is removed in the state of *īhā*. For example, we may say to ourselves that the sound is sweet and not harsh. This state of thinking in which the properties of the object are reflected upon with a view to removing doubt is called *īhā*. Thus, *īhā* is not doubt but it is the state which comes after doubt. It would seem from the above account that, according to the Jainas, in every perception there is a state of doubt which comes between *avagraha* and *īhā*. But we do not always feel the presence of this doubt. Hemacandra explains this as being due to quick succession of stages.[2] This *īhā* is not doubt but it is a mental state in which the properties of the object are reflected upon with a view to removing doubt. Umāsvāti gives different synonyms of *īhā* as *ūhā*, *tarka vicāraṇā* and *jijñāsā*.[3]

Avāya : After *avagraha* and *īhā* there comes the stage of *avāya*. In this stage we get a clear cognition of the object. *Avāya* is the final determination of the specific nature of the object, which takes the form, "this is so and so, and not of the other kind." In other words, *avāya* may be regarded as perceptual judgment. Vādideva and Hemacandra describe *avāya* as the determination of the specific feature of the object cognised in the stage of *īhā*.[4] For example, on hearing a sound a man ascertains that it must be of a conchshell and not of a horn, because it is sweet and not harsh. Thus *avāya* is the perceptual judgment.

Dhāraṇā : *Dhāraṇā* is the last stage of perception. It is

1. *anvayavyatirekarūpaviśeṣaparyālocanarūpā mateḥ ceṣṭā īhā, PM*, I.1.17.
2. *iha cāvagrahehayorantarāle abhyaste'pi viṣaye saṁśayajñānamastyeva āśubhāvāttu nopalakṣyate, ibid.*
3. *TB*, I.15.
4. *PM*, I.1.28.

the cause of the memory of the object which is apprehended in *avāya*. For example, in *avāya* there is a final determination that the sound I hear must be of a shell; and whenever I would hear the sound in the future, I would remember that it is the same sound which I had heard before. This stage of retention of the past experience is called *dhāraṇā*. Umāsvāti defines *dhāraṇā* as the final determination of the object and the cause of the retention of that object.[1] Akalaṅka defines *dhāraṇā* as the condition of recollection—a condition called *saṁskāra* (trace). It is the nature of knowledge.[2] The experience of *avāya* is retained in the form of a cognitional trace and this cognitional trace makes possible the recollection of the past experiences. In this sense, *dhāraṇā* is the cause of memory; it is the *saṁskāra* or the trace due to which memory is possible. Hemacandra defines *dhāraṇā* thus:[3] "*dhāraṇā* is the cause of memory." He holds that *dhāraṇā* is the cause of memory; it is the *saṁskāra* or the trace. *Saṁskāra* is of the nature of cognition; if it were not cognition, then there could arise no knowledge from it, or knowledge cannot be produced by it. *Dhāraṇā* is the existence of knowledge for a definite and indefinite time, while *avāya* etc., are momentary.

2. *The Relation Between the Stages*

Now, a question may arise, are the four stages of empirical perception different or non-different? What is the relation between them? The Jainas hold that the four stages of empirical perception are neither completely different nor completely non-different. There is *bhedābheda* relation amongst them. In one aspect they are different, and in another they are non-different. They are *different* in the sense that they manifest different aspects of the object.[4] Their natures are different. For example, *avagraha* manifests the object while *īhā* removes the doubt about it. Again, it is not necessary that every process of perceptual knowledge should pass through all the stages. Sometimes the process stops only at the first or the second stage;

1. *dhāraṇā pratipattiravadhāraṇamavasthānaṁ niścayo avagamaḥ avabodhaḥ*, *TB*, I.15.
2. *smṛtihetudhāraṇāsaṁskāra*, *AGT*, p. 2-3.
3. *smṛtiheturdhāraṇā*, *PM*, I.1.29.
4. *vastunobhinnābhinnadharmasya prakāśakatvāt*, *PNT*, p. 27.

at others, the process goes right up to the fourth stage.[1] It is possible that the subject does not want to go through the details of the object and then the process of empirical perception may stop with the first or the second stage and does not pass through all the four stages. This also proves that the stages are different. If they were completely non-different then in the process of empirical perception they all would be necessary.

On the other hand, the four stages are *non-different*, because they belong to one and the same process. The process is not different, it is an activity of consciousness and there is a succession of stages one after another. Therefore, they are not completely different. The subject (consciousness)and the object are the same, but the activity has different stages, just as a man is the same but he passes through different stages from his childhood to old age. The stages are the different results of the one process, therefore they are not completely different.[2] They come one after another in a succession, although the succession is not known. Thus, the stages are different and non-different in two aspects. In their natures they are different . But, as constituting one process they are non-different; every stage is a part of the whole process.

Further, in the process of empirical knowledge either there are two, or three, or all the four stages but they come one after another, at first *avagraha*, then *īhā*, then *avāya*, and then *dhāraṇā*. Every empirical knowledge begins from *avagraha*. Although the process may stop at the first or the second stage but there is a succession of their number; the second cannot come before the first or the third cannot come before the second.

3. *Nirvikalpa and Savikalpa Pratyakṣa*

In most systems of Indian Philosophy perception is divided in two modes, namely, *nirvikalpa* and *savikalpa pratyakṣa*. Though most of the systems accept these two modes, yet there is much difference regarding the exact nature and validity of the two. Some hold that both *nirvikalpa* and *savikalpa* are valid knowledge, while some others accept only one of them as valid.

1. *asāmastyena api utpadyamānatvāt, ibid.*
2. *PNT* (Hindi tr.), p. 20.

According to the Buddhists, *nirvikalpa* is the only type of valid perception. They hold that there is non-conceptual data in perceptual knowledge; all perceptual knowledge is free from concept, they are merely sensuous. According to them, what is given is a unique individual, there is no class, name, quality of the object. Thus class, name etc. are constructions of mind and do not belong to the given object. Thus *nirvikalpa* perception is a knowledge of the given and not the modification by any class or name etc. of the object. It is only the pure sensation. Again, it cannot be expressed in words, because there are no concepts in *Nirvikalpa* perception, though it is a pure sensation, yet it is valid. The Buddhists hold that *savikalpa* perception is not valid because it has the conceptual element in it and because it is not due to given object.

According to the *Sāṁkhya* and the *Bhāṭṭa Mīmāṁsakas*, *nirvikalpa* and *savikalpa* both are equally valid and necessary modes of perception. According to them, *nirvikalpa* is the cognition which arises at the first moment of the contact between sense and the object. The object appears as an individual, there is no difference between the universal and particular qualities of the object. In other words, this knowledge is not definite, it does not apprehend its object as being of this kind or that kind. It is like the perception of a child or a dumb person. And, therefore, it cannot be expressed in language. In *nirvikalpa* perception there is simple apprehension in which the object appears merely as 'something', there is no definition of something. It is judgment without words. But *Savikalpa* perception is predicative knowledge of an object. In it, the knowledge of the indefinite character of an object is determined, and analysed into the universal and particular and the two are related in prediction. Thus, according to the *Sāṁkhya* and the *Bhāṭṭa Mīmāṁsakas*, *nirvikalpa* and *savikalpa* are two stages of perception of the same fact.

According to the *Nyāya-Vaiśeṣikas* also, *nirvikalpa* and *savikalpa* both are the necessary modes of perception. They hold that in *nirvikalpa* perception there is knowledge of both the universal and the particular qualities of the object. But these are apprehended in isolation in the *nirvikalpa* perception. For example, in *nirvikalpa* perception we acquire knowledge of an 'apple', not as an 'apple', but as the grasping of a certain colour, taste, smell etc. It is an apprehension of the object as something but not related to a class and called by a name. Thus, it is the knowledge of an existence and attribute of an object but it cannot be expressed in word. In *savikalpa*, an object is known as related to certain qualities. The object is the same, in *nirvikalpa* and in *savikalpa*, but in *nirvikalpa* there is no such relation between the object and the class, name etc. and so it cannot be expressed in words or in a judgment. But in *savikalpa* the objects and its class, name etc. are apprehended in the subject-predicate-relation. *Nirvikalpa* is the first and necessary state for *savikalpa*.

While the Buddhists accept only the *nirvikalpa* perception as valid knowledge, the grammarians (*śābdikas*) hold that *nirvikalpa* perception is not real. According to them all objects are connected with words. All knowledge and our ideas are expressed in prepositions. There can be no such knowledge as *nirvikalpa*, which is independent of verbal expression. Therefore, all perception is *savikalpa* or determinate knowledge of objects, as qualified by the attributes expressed in words.

The Jainas, however, do not distinguish perception as *savikalpa* and *nirvikalpa*. But they recognise four stages of perception. Of these, the first stage, *avagraha* may be compared with *Nirvikalpa* perception. Some Jaina logicians, like Akalaṅka, hold it as determinate knowledge and others as indeterminate. But whether it is determinate or indeterminate, it is the first stage of perception, in the same way as *nirvikalpa* is regarded as the first stage of perception.

In the logical literature of the Jainas, perception is taken to be only determinate or *savikalpa*. Determination is a criterion of true knowledge. The Jainas do not accept the Buddhist view of *nirvikalpa* perception. In the following sections we will try to explain the Jaina criticism of the *nirvikalpa* of the Buddhists. The Jainas also reject the view of the *śābdikas* that there is an identity between the word and the object. The criticism of the *śābdikas* will be explained in section 5 of this chapter.

4. *Buddhist View of Nirvikalpa*

According to the Jainas, the criterion of right knowledge

is determinateness. If it is not determinate it cannot contradict error, doubt etc.[1] The Buddhists do not accept this view; they hold that determinateness is not a criterion of right knowledge, for it would then be conceptual. All conceptual knowledge is, according to them, false. They believe in pure sensation as valid knowledge, because it is free from all verbal expression. It is a pure sensation because the object of knowledge is unique and momentary, The verbal expression is not possible for a momentary object. If there is any verbal expression, it would be based on the memory of the object which was sensed a few moments before. Thus, verbal expression cannot belong to right knowledge. If right knowledge is based on verbal expression then there would be a lapse of time between sensation and its verbal expression. At first there is sensation and then the verbal expression, which is based on memory. Thus, there is no value of this expression; it is like a dead body.

The Jainas reject the Buddhist view that there is no verbal expression or concept in perceptual knowledge. They say that it is always seen that there is verbal expression in all perceptual knowledge; for example, on seeing blue one says "this is blue". There is no knowledge without any verbal expression. Thus, according to the Jainas, all perceptual knowledge possesses some verbal expression. Otherwise, even non-conscious things would be able to know.[2]

The Jainas contend that we experience only the *savikalpaka* and no *nirvikalpaka*. The Buddhist may reply that although both are present the two are wrongly taken to be one. The Jainas however, point out that two things may be taken as one only when their distinction is apprehended on some other occasion. In the present case, we never apprehend *nirvikalpaka* and *savikalpaka* separately; therefore, we cannot say that there are two things which are taken to be one.[3]

The Buddhists might still argue that the two are taken to be one because they take place simultaneously (*yugapad*). The Jainas point out that we do not always take to be one all these

1. *tad vyavasāyasvabhāvaṁ samāropaparipanthitvāt pramāṇatvād vā*, *PNT*, I.7.
2. *SR*, I.6.
3. *Ibid.*

knowledges which arise together. For example, one may have a visual, a tactual, and an auditory perception in the same time, but no one ever fails to apprehend their difference. The Buddhists might reply that in this example the objects of the various knowledges are different. The Jainas reply that even in the case of *nirvikalpaka* and *savikalpaka* the objects are different, for the object of the former is momentary and the object of the latter is the sensation.[1]

Again, the Jainas argue that if the Buddhists accept the distinction between *nirvikalpaka* and *savikalpaka*, although this is not apprehended, then why do they reject the *Sāṁkhya* distinction between *buddhi* and consciousness on the very same ground.[2] The Jainas point out that the difference between the two may not be apprehended either due to the similarity between them or because one of them overpowers the other.[3] But what could be the similarity? Is it because the objects are identical or is it because the two knowledges are of the same nature? The objects are not identical, as we have seen before. The second alternative is also not acceptable, for in that case we should also not apprehend the distinction between a sensation of blue and sensation of yellow, for as sensation they are alike.[4]

Shall we then say that the two are not distinguished because one of them overpowers the other?[5] The Buddhists hold that the *savikalpaka* overpowers the *nirvikalpaka*. The Jainas would ask: Why should not the *nirvikalpaka* overpower the *savikalpaka*? The Buddhists might reply that the *savikalpaka* is stronger than *nirvikalpaka*. The Jainas ask: what does its strength consist in? It cannot be due to its object, for the object of *nirvikalpaka* is also the object of *savikalpaka*, otherwise the *savikalpaka* would be a completely different *pramāṇa*. Shall we then say that the *savikalpaka* is stronger because it is judgmental? But then where does its judgmental character lie? Does it lie in the nature of the knowledge or in the nature of the object? Not the former, for every knowledge, according to

1. *SR*, I. 6.
2. *Ibid.*
3. *PKM*, p. 28.
4. *Ibid.*, p. 29.
5. *Ibid.*

the Buddhists, is self-revealing and this self-revelation is not judgmental. If the judgmental character concerns the object, then every *vikalpa* would be both judgmental and non-judgmental and this would give rise to many difficulties.[1]

Again, what is meant by judgment of identity (*ekatvādhyavasāya*) between the two? (i) Does it mean that the two knowledges have the same object? Or (ii) does it mean that one of the knowledges takes on the object of the other? Or (iii) is one knowledge superimposed on the other?[2]

(i) The first alternative is not tenable, for the object of one is the universal and that of the other the particular. The (*dṛśya*) and the *vikalpa* cannot be mistaken to be one. If the two are apprehended, they cannot, like a pillar and jar, ever be confused. Further, how can the two be known? They cannot be known by *nirvikalpaka* alone nor by *savikalpaka* alone. They cannot be known by a third knowledge, for this third knowledge must be either *nirvikalpaka* or *savikalpaka*. If the two are unknown, then also they cannot be mistaken to be one. All superimposition is due to similarity, but there is no similarity between the *dṛśya* and the *vikalpa*. The one is real and the other is unreal. Therefore, the two knowledges cannot be taken to be one in the first sense.

(ii) Is it possible that one of the knowledges takes the other for its object? If the two knowledges are simultaneous, then they are indifferent of each other and the one cannot be the object of the other. If the two knowledges are in different times, then also it is not possible. For being momentary, when the later knowledge arises, the former would disappear.

(iii) The third alternative is also not acceptable.[3] Is the *nirvikalpaka* superimposed on the *savikalpaka* or is the *savikalpaka* superimposed on the *nirvikalpaka*? In the first case, there would be no *savikalpaka* judgment for all knowledge would become *nirvikalpaka*. In the second case, all knowledge would become *savikalpaka* so that we cannot even speak of *nirvikalpaka*. The Buddhists hold that the property of *vaiśadya*, which belongs

1. *PKM*, p. 30; *SR*, I. 6

2. *kasya ca anayorekatvādhyavasāyaḥ kimekaviṣayatvam, anyatareṇānyatarasya viṣayikaraṇaṁ vā, paratretarasya adhyāropo vā*, *PKM*, p. 30.

3. *SR*, I.6.; *PKM*, p. 30.

to the *nirvikalpaka*, is wrongly transferred to *savikalpaka* and so the later seems clear and distinct. The *avaiśadya* belonging to *savikalpaka* is wrongly transferred to *nirvikalpaka*. If the *vaiśadya* of *nirvikalpaka* overpowers the *avaiśadya* of *savikalpaka*, then how could the same *avaiśadya* be again transferred to *nirvikalpaka* ? Or, if the *avaiśadya* of *savikalpaka* overpowers the *vaiśadya* of *nirvikalpaka* then how can the latter *vaiśadya* be again transferred to the former.[1]

Even if we accept that the property of *vikalpa* is overpowered by the property of *nirvikalpaka*, still we have to explain why this takes place. It cannot take place simply because the two knowledges are simultaneous, for in that case, if the thought of a horse and the perception of a cow happen together, then the former would become as clear as the latter.[2]

The Buddhists may reply that the two having different objects, the property of one cannot be transferred to the other. But in that case, if we hear a sound at a particular time and at the same time infer its momentariness, then the clarity (*vaiśadya*) of the first ought to be transferred to the inference. The Buddhists may reply that this does happen because the two knowledges arise out of different factors. The Jainas would say that in that case no *vikalpa* could arise from the same factors as those of *nirvikalpaka*. The *vikalpaka* arises from *vaiśadya* while *nirvikalpaka* arises from the contact of the sense organs; therefore the property of *nirvikalpaka* can never be transferred to *savikalpaka*.

Who makes the judgment of identity between the two ?[3] The *nirvikalpaka* cannot do it, for it is non-judgmental and unerring; *savikalpaka* cannot do it, for it does not have the *nirvikalpaka* for its object. Why do the Buddhists regard *savikalpaka* perception as invalid ? Is it because (1) it lacks a clear and distinct form (*spaṣṭākāra vikalatvāt*) ? Or, (2) is it because it apprehends what is already apprehended (*grahītagrāhitvāt*)? Or, (3) is it because it leads to activity with respect to something which is non-existent (*asatipravartanāt*) ? Or, (4) is it because it is incapable of leading to the attainment of what is good and

1. *SR*, I. 6; *PKM*, p. 30.
2. *Ibid*; *Ibid*, p. 31.
3. *SR*, p. 52-57: *PKM*, p. 31-38.

rejection of what is bad (*hitāhita prāptiparihārasamarthatvāt*) ? Or, (5) is it because it is something contradicted (*kadācidvisaṁvādāt*) ? Or, (6) is it because it does not negate error (*samāropasya niṣedhakatvāt*) ? Or, (7) is it because it is unfit for practical use (*vyavahārānupayogāt*) ? Or, (8) is it because it does not apprehend the more particular (*svalakṣaṇāgocaratvāt*)? Or, (9) is it because it manifests only that which is related to word (*śabdasaṁsargayogyapratibhāsatvāt*) ? Or, (10) is it because it arises due to śabda (*śabdaprabhāvatvāt*) ?

Not (1), because *savikalpaka* is known to be clear and distinct and also because the same difficulty would invalidate inference as well. Not (2), because inference would be invalid on the same ground as the object of inference is already known in the knowledge of *vyāpti* and also in the knowledge of the *yogīs*. Not (3), because even the object of *nirvikalpaka* is non-existent at the time of knowledge. Not (4), for it is well known that *savikalpaka* perception leads to attainment of the good and rejection of the bad, and if sometimes it does not do so, that is also the cause with *nirvikalpaka*. Not (5), because *nirvikalpa* also may sometimes be contradicted as in the case of the perception of a person with diseased eyes. Not (6), because the substratum of error is not the object of *vikalpaka*. Not (7), because all practical activity is based on *savikalpaka*. Not (8), because inference also would be invalid on the same ground. Not (9), because the same defect also invalidates inference. Not (10), because a *nirvikalpaka* perception of a sound particular (*śabdalakṣaṇa*) would be invalid on the same ground.

To sum up, the distinction between truth and error is to be found as much in *nirvikalpaka* as in *savikalpaka*. There can be *nirvikalpaka* of the double moon if there is some defect in the eyes. It may be noted that the possibility in error in *nirvikalpaka* is not admitted by any other school of philosophy.[1]

5. *Bhartṛhari's View*

According to Bhartṛhari, there is no knowledge without connection with words. All knowledge is intermingled (*anuviddha*) with words. The followers of Bhartṛhari distinguish

1. All arguments are taken from *Syādvāda-Ratnākara*, Part I.

between three kinds of speech. The first is that which is used by us in the form of alphabets and produced by efforts in succession, it is called *vaikharī*. The second is the inner speech, having succession but not expressed in audible sounds; it is known as *madhyamā*. Finally, there is speech which is of the nature of consciousness, which is self-revealing and which is free from all the succession and distinctions; it is known as *paśyantī*. Speech in this last sense, according to Bhartṛhari, is the eternal *Brahman*. All distinctions are superimposed on the reality due to ignorance. That is why all knowledge is ultimately nothing but *śabda*.

The Jaina would ask : What is meant by this intermingling of knowledge with *śabda*. Does it mean a special kind of connection between the two, as is found between mercury and a metal ? But if this were so, then there are two different things, *śabda* and knowledge. This would go against the thesis of *śabdādvaita-vāda*.

Does it mean that there is *tādātmya* or identity between knowledge and *śabda*, just as there is identity between a piece of cloth and its blue colour ? If knowledge and words were identical, then knowledge would become unconscious like word. Again, if a word is the same as knowledge, then words uttered by one cannot be heard by another.

How is the identity between the two known ? It cannot be known by perception because perception apprehends *śabda* as distinct from itself. It cannot be apprehended by inference because such an inference would be contradicted by perception.

Bhartṛhari may argue that the identity between knowledge and *śabda* can be proved on the ground of the identity between the word (*śabda*) and the object (*artha*). Let us, therefore, examine whether this identity between word and object can be maintained.

Bhartṛhari holds that there is the identity between the knowledge and the word, that is, all our knowledges of things are expressed in words. And this identity can be proved on the ground of the identity between the word (*śabda*) and the object (*artha*). Thus Bhartṛhari says that there is an identity between the word and the object, because every object is denoted by a word.

The Jainas ask as to what is meant by the identity between

the word and the object? Identity means possessing the nature of that. In the present case, with whom does the word possess identity? Since there is no object other than word, or no word other than object, one cannot speak of identity between them.

Again, the Jainas point out that there is no perceptual knowledge of such identity. For example, in visual perception one sees only the object as the jar, cloth etc., but he cannot see the words 'jar', 'cloth' etc. And in auditory perception one hears only the words, 'jar', 'cloth' etc., but he cannot see the objects. The identity cannot be proved by inference also, because inference is based on perception.

There is no identity between the word and the object, because these are the objects of different sense organs. For example, the eye cannot manifest the object of taste. If colour and sound were perceived by the same sense organ then we need not accept many sense organs; only one sense organ will do.

The Jainas point out that it is not true to say that when the *śabda* is heard, the object also is known. It is possible to apprehend an object without relating it to any word. If it is *śabda*, even in such apparently non-linguistic knowledge, then just as in the state of deep sleep, subtle sound is present. But this account is not tenable. They cannot give a good explanation of why and how the subtle sound becomes gross sound.

Since there is no identity between the word and the object, there is also no identity between the word and the knowledge. In fact, if the word and the knowledge were identical, then Bhartṛhari's statement that all knowledge is mingled (*anuviddha*) with the word would become pointless.

They gave the example of *vṛkṣatva* and *śiṁśapātva*. This example however does not possess the *sādhya*, which is complete identity. The two, *vṛkṣatva* and *śiṁśapātva* are not completely identical. There are trees possessing but not possessing *śiṁśapātva*. The example also does not possess the *hetu*, for there is no necessary rule that one who perceives *vṛkṣatva* also perceives *śiṁśapātva*.

CHAPTER VI

JAINA THEORY OF PERCEPTUAL ERROR

The Jainas define *pramā* as the knowledge, which is *vyavasāyātmaka* (judgmental or determinate). It may be argued that this adjective is useless, since there is, in fact, no error or doubt which it can serve to exclude. The Jainas point out that this is not correct, because doubt is possible. Everybody feels doubt in everyday life. One who questions the possibility of doubt is himself making use of a doubt, which is absurd. How is one to disprove the existence of doubt ? Does one know that there is no doubt because of the non-existence of its causes, or because of the non-existence of its peculiar qualities, or because of the non-existence of its peculiar object [1]? The first argument is not good, for every doubt has some causes of its existence. These are : the perception of the common qualities and non-perception of the specific qualities of an object. Again, doubt arises due to the *saṁskāras* and *karma*. Thus, doubt has its own causes. The second argument is also wrong, because the peculiar nature of doubt is experienced by anyone in day to day life. The third argument is also not correct, because every doubt has its object, there is no non-existence of the object of doubt : for example, in doubt the object appears as having two or more properties. In the case of the doubt, "is this a man or a tree ", the object is the general character of uprightness, not known to be determined either by "manhood" or by "treeness".

Thus, the existence of doubt is proved and by the same arguments the possibility of *viparyaya* or error may also be proved.

1. *Akhyātivāda*

The *Cārvāka* theory of error is called *akhyāti*[2], for according to the *Cārvākas* nothing is apprehended in *viparyaya* or

1. *PKM*, p. 48.
2. Prabhācandra uses the word *akhyāti* for the Cārvāka's theory of error. But generally the word *akhyāti* is used for the *Prābhākaras'* theory of non-apprehension of the difference between a perception and a memory. The *Cārvāka* theory is usually called *asatkhyāti*.

error. They ask as what would be the object of the knowledge, in which one wrongly perceives water, where it is not. Is it water, or the non-existence of water, or mirage, or another thing? In appearance of water in mirage, the object is not water, for if this were so then this knowledge could not be called error. The non-existence of water would not be the object of this knowledge, because, knowledge has always some positive object. The mirage itself would not be the object of the knowledge, because if the mirage appears as mirage then this knowledge would not be a *viparyaya* or error. The mirage would not seem as water, because one thing does not appear like another, the jar does not appear as a cloth. Thus, the *viparyaya* or error has no object.

The Jainas would ask, if there is no object of error, then how could an error have the specific form : 'This is water', or 'This is silver'? And what do the *Cārvākas* mean by *akhyāti*? Do they mean by it the non-existence of the object? If they mean by it non-existence of the object, then there would be no difference between *bhrānti* and *suṣupti* because in the state of *suṣupti* there is non-existence of the object. Thus, the argument that in *viparyaya* there is non-existence of object is not correct.

2. *Asatkhyātivāda*[1]

The advocates of the *asatkhyāti* theory may argue that the object that appears in error, *if regarded as real*, is non-existent. The form of the silver which appears, is absent in the shell. According to the *Mādhyamikas*, the knowledge of silver in the shell is erroneous because it manifests the non-existent silver as existent. The Jainas reject this and point out that the non-existent object cannot appear at all, just as the sky-flower does not appear. The appearance of the non-existent object would be a contradiction. Only existent things appear. If the object of *viparyaya* would be *asat* or non-existent then there would be no difference amongst the different kinds of errors.

1. *PKM*, p. 49.

3. *Prasiddhārthakhyātivāda*[1]

According to the *Sāṁkhya* view of error, it is not non-existence of the object but the real object is apprehended in error. The apprehended object is not non-existent, but it appears as a real object. There is no contradiction here; just as one perceives his own palm, so also in error one perceives a real object. One sees water in mirage. It is another thing that afterwards he does not get water and his knowledge of the existence of water becomes false. A thing may appear first and may afterwards disappear, but this disappearance should not be the cause of the non-existence of the thing. For example, the lightning appears in the sky and then disappears, but this does not mean that lightning is a non-existent thing. Thus, in error also, the object cannot be called non-existent. The Jainas reject this view, and point out that if the object of error would be accepted as such, then there would be no difference between the object of error and the object of true knowledge; the object of error would be apprehended like the object of true knowledge. Then one should see real water in mirage. The Jainas ask that if one saw real water in mirage then he must be able to find some marks of water afterwards. But this is not so in practice. In practice, one sees water in mirage but afterwards he finds that his knowledge of the existence of water was wrong; there was no water but due to some special causes he saw water. If really there was water, then afterwards also one would be able to find some marks of its presence.

4. *Ātmakhyātivāda*[2]

According to the *Yogācāras*, all objects are only ideas; there is no external reality. There is no difference between the knowledge, knower and the object. Knowledge has the form of the object. The knowledge of silver in shell is also subjective, but due to *avidyā* this subjective form appears as external.

1. PKM,. p. 49-50.
2. *Ibid.*, p. 50.

Prabhācandra points out that the *Ātmakhyātivādin* can be correct only if we also accept that knowledge has the form of the object, and that knowledge knows only itself. Both these properties are rejected by the Jainas. Further, if all knowledge knows only its own form, then there would be no distinction between true knowledge and false knowledge. Again, if the form of the silver is a form of knowledge, it would be impossible for it to appear outside, just as pleasure and pain never appear to be outside. The knower would never have the *pravṛtti* to acquire, for the inner states are constantly changing. If the Buddhists say that what is inner and changing appears as outer and permanent then the Jainas point out that in that case the Buddhists would have to accept *viparīta-khyāti*.

5. *Anirvacanīya khyātivāda*

According to *anirvacanīyakhyātivāda*, the object of error is called *anirvacanīya* or indefinable. The object of knowledge is apprehended as such. In knowledge of water, water is apprehended as water, not as another thing. Thus, in error, if water is apprehended as water, then there would be no error or false knowledge. On the other hand, if water is apprehended as not water (as non-existent), then it would be impossible, for how could a non-existent entity appear ? If water is apprehended as existent at the same time, then there would be contradiction, which is not possible. Thus, the object in error cannot be defined either as existent or as non-existent; therefore it should be *anirvacanīya* or indefinable.

The Jainas reject this view of *anirvacanīya* and point out that the water is apprehended as real not as something *anirvacanīya*[1]. The *pravṛtti* of the person who sees it is directed towards real water. One cannot have such behavior towards water that is *anirvacanīya*. The existence of water in mirage is apprehended in a particular place and time; how can then it be called *anirvacanīya* or indefinable ? What is apprehended should not be called indefinable. If the *Advaitists* say that though the water is in itself *anirvacanīya*, yet it appears as real, in that case the Jainas point out that the *Advaitists* must accept *viparītakhyāti*, for one thing is appearing as another.

1. PKM., p. 51.

6. *Smṛtipramoṣavāda*[1]

According to the *Prābhākara Mīmāṁsakas,* in knowledge of a shell as a silver, there is not one knowledge but two knowledges. Because, two different effects are produced by two different causes. In the judgment, "This is silver", 'this' and 'silver' are two different knowledges having two different causes. Knowledge of 'this' is caused by perception, and that of 'silver' caused by memory. The sense-organs cannot perceive an absent object; the presence of a defect (*doṣa*) in the causes can only prevent the production of the effect, but a defective cause cannot produce a new effect. For example, if a seed of an apple tree is defective, it will not produce an apple tree, but it cannot go on to produce an orange tree. Therefore, there are two knowledges, the knowledge of 'this' and the knowledge of 'silver'. The shell is apprehended as something present, but the 'silver' is not present; it appears in the shell due to the memory of the past perception of silver. In the knowledge of shell as silver the difference between the memory and the perception is not apprehended. The memory of the past experience of silver and the present experience of the shell are mixed up and the shell appears as silver. In this case of error the memory of silver does not appear as memory. This is called by the *Prābhākaras* as *smṛtipramoṣa* or suppression of memory. As a consequence, the man who is under illusion does not know that he is remembering. From this non-apprehension of the distinction between perception and memory arises the pravṛtti of the person.

The Jainas reject the *Prābhākara* view. They held that in the case of *doṣa* it is not true that the presence of a *doṣa* cannot produce a new effect. But the defect or *doṣa* of the eyes is the cause of wrong knowledge. It is the *doṣa* or the defect of sense organs due to which a non-existent object seems as existent. In the knowledge of a shell as a silver, there is no *asatkhyāti*, but the error is due to the similarity of shell and silver. A perception of a sky-flower cannot be due to such similarities. There is not *ātmakhyāti* also, because the silver is not a form of the knowledge. The knowledge of the silver is rather caused by *saṁskāra* together with *doṣa* and similarity.

The knowledge of silver in a shell is not "it is that silver" because silver is apprehended as present. Now can the ex-

1. PKM, p. 53-58.

perience of the past be apprehended as that of the present ? This difficulty is the same with the Prabhākaras also. Thus, how would, in *smṛti-pramoṣa*, the past experience be apprehended in the present object ? Though there is the similarity between the shell and the silver yet the shell cannot be called 'this is silver', because there is no real silver and it also cannot be said, "there is no silver", because the shell appears as the silver. There is no *vivekakhyāti* which presupposes the *bheda* or difference between the 'this' and 'silver'. For example, in the judgment 'this is a pot', there is no difference between 'this' and 'pot'. Thus, the defect of the sense-organ would be the cause of wrong knowledge.

The Jainas ask, what is meant by *smṛtipramoṣa*[1] ? Is it the absence of memory, or is it the apprehension of the other (other than the remembered silver), or is it the apprehension of the past object as present ? Or is it an apprehension in which memory and present perception are mixed up without distinction like milk and water?

The first alternative would not be right for if the absence of memory would be *smṛtipramoṣa* then how can the silver perceived in the past be apprehended in the present ? If in such cases, the memory is absent, then there would be no difference between *smṛtipramoṣa* and states of swoon or deep sleep.

The *smṛtipramoṣa* is also not apprehension of something other than the remembered silver, for if it were so, then it may be asked, is this apprehension in the same time as the memory, or does it take place after the memory ? In the former case, if there is perception of a jar during the memory, there should be *smṛtipramoṣa*, which is absurd. If the appearance of the other takes place after the memory, it cannot bring about *pramoṣa* of that memory. For if it could do so, then every succeeding knowledge could bring about a *pramoṣa* of the preceding memory.

Nor can *smṛtipramoṣa* be apprehension of the past silver as present, for in that case, there ought to be absence of clearness in the memory of the silver, as in the case of the other memories. But this is not so.

Smṛtipramoṣa cannot also be the mixture of memory with

1. PKM, p. 56.

perception without distinction, as in the case of milk and water. What is meant by non-distinction? Is it the apprehension of two real but different things as identical? Or is it a relation of *saṁśleṣa* between the two? Or is it origination together? In the first case, one has to accept *viparītakhyāti*, which is the Jaina view. The second alternative is not possible for there cannot be relation of *saṁśleṣa* between two knowledges. In the last case, any two knowledges arising together could be undistinguished but this is not so.

The knowledge of the double moon is not memory, for in that case there should not be a relation of universal co-presence and co-absence between its knowledge and the sense-organs.

According to the theory of *smṛtipramoṣa*, there cannot be a correcting knowledge. Where the error is corrected, we say, "this is not silver". We do not say, "the appearance of silver was a memory".

7. *Anyathākhyāti or Viparītakhyāti*

According to this view, an illusory experience is not a complex of perception and memory, as the Prabhākaras hold, but it is a single perception. Error is the apprehension of an object as other than what it is. This view is called *anyathākhyāti* of *viparītakhyāti* and it is accepted by the *Naiyāyikas*, Kumārila and the Jainas.

"According to the Nyāya, illusion is a misplaced fact. All the factors of an illusory perception are real and perceived facts, but they are brought into a wrong relation. In the illusory perception of silver, for example, we have an actual perception of a certain locus and some silver, both as real facts. The error arises because the silver perceived at a different time and place, is related to the time and place occupied by the perceived locus, namely, the shell"[1].

Kumārila holds that error consists in malobservation. Due to wrong apprehension we do not note the peculiar qualities of a shell as distinguished from the silver, and at the same time by the glow etc. (of the shell) we take the shell as the silver, which we have seen elsewhere. The silver is not utterly non-existent, because it exists elsewhere and it is the memory of it,

1. Chatterjee, S. C., *Nyāya Theory of Knowledge*, p. 41.

think of the shell as silver. Thus, the error is due to the determination of one presentation by another given through association and memory (*jātyasaṁskārāt*).

Prabhācandra accepts the view of *viparītakhyāti*. He holds that in the knowledge of tree as man, the error consists in wrong apprehension of the qualities of the object. The error arises due to the defects of eyes or some other causes. Thus the Jainas accept the view of *viparītakhyāti*.

PART THREE

NON-SENSUOUS PERCEPTION

CHAPTER VII

IDEA OF NON-SENSUOUS PERCEPTION IN PHILOSOPHY

The concept of non-sensuous perception is found in most of the systems of Indian philosophy. The non-sensuous perception is called *atīndriyapratyakṣa*. It is intuitive experience; it arises in the self. In the first place, such perception is not caused in the ordinary way. The sense-organs do not play a role in its production. Secondly, there is no limitation of space, time and place for it. One possesses the experience, can know the objects of the past, present, future, far and near.

Again, the systems, which believe in *atīndriyapratyakṣa* accept that it arises in the self directly when the ignorance is destroyed by the regular practice of mental and bodily discipline. And in the state of purification or perfection, the self shines by the light of great knowledge, and there arise some supernormal powers or the *siddhi* or *labdhi* in the self. Those are not any type of miracles, but the power of the self itself which arises by the destruction of ignorance.

The aim of the *yogī* is not to acquire the supernormal power. He practises for his purification and to get freedom from the bondage of the world.

1. *Nyāya Theory of Alaukika Pratyakṣa*

The modern *Naiyāyikas* classified perception into two types, *laukika* or ordinary perception and *alaukika* or extra-ordinary perception. The first type of perception is based on the sense object contact. In the second type of perception, the objects are not actually present to the senses, but are experienced through an extra-ordinary medium. All the various kinds of extra ordinary sense object contacts are called *alaukika sannikarṣa*. Extra-ordinary perception is of three kinds, namely, *sāmānya-lakṣaṇa jñānalakṣaṇa* and *yogaja*.

(a) *Sāmānya-lakṣaṇa-pratyakṣa* is the perception of a whole class of object through the perception of its generic property, (*sāmānya*). When one perceives an object as a pot, he judges it as belonging to the class of pot; thus, the perception of one pot implies the perception of all pots. According to the *Naiyāyikas,* when we perceive one pot, we perceive the universal 'potness' as its defining property. It is the perception of the universal 'potness' in the present pot. This universal serves as the medium through which all members of the same class are also perceived. We have a perception of all pots of all times and of all places by the perception of one pot. Only one does not perceive all these pots (excepting the present one) in their specific characters; one only perceives them in their generic character of potness[1].

(b) *Jñānalakṣaṇa*—On seeing a piece of sandalwood, one may say, 'I see a piece of fragrant sandalwood'. Ordinarily, one does not see fragrance, one smells it. But in the present case, one has a direct visual experience of the fragrance of the sandalwood. How is this possible? Here the past knowledge of fragrance brings about the present visual perception of it. There is no ordinary apprehension of fragrance. It is an indirect and extra-ordinary perception in which a past knowledge leads to the present perception of its own object. Thus, it may be called an extraordinary perception, which is not based on the direct contact between the object and its sense organ[2].

(c) *Yogaja*—It is the intuitive perception of all objects, past, present, future and distant. It is due to a special quality (or power) which arises (in the self) by the practice of *Yoga*. Those who have attained spiritual perfection, attain the knowledge, through their mind, of the *ākāśa*, of the *aṇu*, and of all the objects of all time; they are called *yuktas*. The *yuktas* have this special power by the practice of *Yoga* and meditation, and it cannot be destroyed. And those who are in the way of perfection and do not possess this power fully are called *yuñjānas*[3].

2. *The Advaita Conception of Brahmajñāna*[4]

According to Śaṁkara, *Brahman* is present in every man and is the universal self in all. *Brahman* is reality but different from

1. Chatterjee, S. C. *op. cit.*, pp. 209-210.
2. *Ibid.*, pp. 218-19.
3. *Kārikāvali*, p. 204.
4. S. Radhakrishnan, *Indian Philosophy* II, 510-13.

the phenomenal world and not sensible. *Brahman* is of the nature of consciousness; knowledge is its essential property. It is *sat* (real), *cit* (consciousness) and *ānanda* (bliss). We cannot attain the knowledge of reality or the Brahman, so long as we are subject to *avidyā* or ignorance. *Vidyā* gives the highest conceptual account of Brahman. The *Brahmānubhava* gives the highest experience of Brahman. This is of two kinds : the first, the experience that 'I am Brahman' (*brahmā'smihitya-nubhavaḥ*), and the second experience arises with reference to the universe, that 'All this is Brahman' (*sarvaṁ khalvidaṁ brahma*).

There is no difference between *Brahman* and *Ātman*. *Ātman* is *Brahman*. The *anubhava* of *Ātman* or the integral experience is a type of intuitional consciousness which may be called the knowledge of *Brahman*, in which the individual self feels the identity with *Ātman* or *Brahman*. It is the inexpressible experience beyond thought and speech. It is *sākṣātkāra* or direct perception of the awareness of the empirical self and the *Ātman*. One can get this intuition of *Ātman* by faith, devotion, meditation, study and by a preparation of mind. It is neither a mere fancy nor a private truth but it is open to all.

3. *Supernormal Powers in Yoga System*[1]

Through the practice of *Yoga*, the *sādhaka* acquires some supernormal powers in particular state of the *yaugika-sādhanā*. These are called *siddhi* or the supernormal powers, and a knowledge of supernormal objects. Through it the *Yogī* or the *Sādhaka* knows the inmost core of objects and reaches the great light of wisdom (*prajñāloka*). He acquires heightened powers of the senses by which he can see and hear at a distance, and have direct knowledge of the past. And the *Yogī* can acquire knowledge of others' mind (*paracittajñānaṁ*). He can know also the past, present and future by the supernormal power. The *Yogī* can make his body invisible also. And by the realisation of the difference between the self and the outer world he gains omniscience.

A *Yogī* can acquire all those supernormal powers by the discipline of body and mind. The aim of a *Yogī* is not to acquire

1. S. Radhakrishnan, *Indian Philosophy* II.366-68.

them but he tries to make perfect his self and to get freedom. According to the *Yoga* system of philosophy, these supernormal powers are not considered as miracles, because they hold that the world open to our senses is not the whole world of nature. Our physical senses do not have the power or capacity to perceive the whole world. The world beyond our capacities has its own science and laws, which are apprehended by the supernormal power of the *Yogī.* A *Yogī* acquires this capacity by discipline and meditation.

4. *Yogi-Pratyakṣa of the Buddhists*

Dharmakīrti defines *yogi-pratyakṣa* as the knowledge which is manifested in the highest state of deep meditation on transcendental reality[1]. Dharmottara's commentary on this suggests that there are three stages or degrees of this transcendental perception. In the first stage, the object begins to be clear (*sphuṭābhatvārambhāvasthā*); this state is called *bhāvanā-prakarṣa.* In the second stage, the *Yogī* apprehends the transcendental reality as if it were covered by a transparent sheath, this stage is called *prakarṣaparyantāvasthā.* The third stage is as vivid perception of the object as in the perception of an *āmalaka* fruit on one's palm. This last stage is the *Yogī's* direct knowledge or the *yogī-pratyakṣa*[2]. It immediately arises in the highest stage of meditation.

Dharmettara says that the *yogī-pratyakṣa* is clear and *nirvikalpa* knowledge[3]. The object of *yogī-pratyakṣa* is *paramārthasat*, or the ultimate reality. According to the Buddhists the unique particular and the non-constructed alone is real[4].

The particular is inexpressible. It is direct apprehension of reality; there is no construction; it is just as the mere sensation or the knowledge of the momentary particular. But this perception is entirely mental, not sensuous[5].

1. *bhūtārthabhāvanāprakarṣaparyantajaṁ yogijñānaṁ ceti*, *Nyāya-Bindu*, p.14.
2. *Ibid.*, p. 15.
3. *sphuṭābhatvādeva ca nirvikalpakam, ibid.*
4. *tasya viṣayaḥ svalakṣaṇaṁ, tadeva paramārthasat, ibid.*, pp. 15-17.
5. This is a kind of perception which is entirely mental, Stcherbatsky, *Buddhist Logic*, II, p. 30.

The Buddhists' *Yogī-pratyakṣa* has also been called omniscience (*sarvajñatā*)[1]. But the nature of it cannot be expressed in words (*anirvacanīya*). Because a common man does not possess the power to explain it. In order to explain it one must be an omniscient. We can only imagine it[2].

1. Stcherbatsky, *Buddhist Logic* II, p. 56.
2. *Ibid.*, II, p. 162.

CHAPTER VIII

THE JAINA THEORY OF NON-SENSUOUS PERCEPTION

1. *The Jaina Theory*

The Jainas classify perception into two types—the *sāṁvyavahārika* and the *mukhya.* The former is empirical perception which depends on the sense-organs and mind. The *mukhya* or the non-sensuous perception is direct knowledge, which arises directly in the self without the help of the sense-organs and mind; we may call it therefore supersensuous perception.

The Jaina theory of knowledge is based on their conception of self. The Jainas hold that the self is omniscient. Knowledge is its essential quality. It possesses infinite knowledge—knowledge of all things and at all times. But due to the obstruction of the *karmic* matter, knowledge is obscured. What is the *karmic* matter and how and why does it obscure the pure self? In order to understand this, it is necessary at first to go through the Jaina metaphysics, because their theory of knowledge is based on their metaphysics.

The Jainas believe in seven *tattvas* or principles : *jīva, ajīva, āśrava, bandha, saṁvara, nirjarā* and *mokṣa*[1].

Here we may try to explain the seven principles of the Jainas.

(1) *The Jīva or the self*—Self is a conscious entity. It possesses infinite knowledge, infinite vision (*darśana*), infinite power and infinite bliss. These are the essential qualities of the self. In its pure condition the four qualities are fully developed in the self.

(2) *Ajīva*—What is other than the *jīva* is *ajīva.* The *jīva* is conscious but *ajīva* is non-conscious. It may be called matter. Every self is essentially pure; matter is the cause of an unclean veil on the self due to which the self cannot shine in its natural conditions. *Jīva* and the matter are mixed up from the beginning-

1. *jīvājīvāśravabandha-saṁvara-nirjarā-mokṣāḥ tattvam, TS,*I.4.

less time. But the veil of matter may be destroyed by the discipline of body and mind, and then the self may come to its natural condition of infinite knowledge and infinite bliss etc.

(3) *Āśrava*—The *āśrava* may be called as the movement of the *karmic* matter. The whole universe is full of *karmic matters*, according to the Jainas. And through the action of body, mind and speech the *karmic* matter is attracted to the self. The movement of the *karmic* matters towards the self is called *āśrava*. It means a door-way or a channel. The passage through which water finds its way into a tank is called *āśrava*. In the same way, the principle through which *karmic* matter flows into the self is called *āśrava*.

The self is effected by *rāga*, *dveṣa*, *rati*, and *moha*, which are the actions of body, speech and mind. These actions are called *yoga*; that is the *kāyayoga*, *vacanayoga* and *manoyoga*. Due to these three forms of *yoga*, *karmic* matter flows into the self; *yoga* is thus the same as *āśrava*[1].

The past matters of the self effect its present activity, and the present activities determine the future of the self. The *karmas* are themselves indifferent, they do not desire to come or to stay, but it is through the actions of self which are done by body, mind and speech, that the *karmic* matters are attracted to the self, just as the iron files are attracted to a magnet.

(4) *Bandha*—The *bandha* may be called the *karmic* bondage. *Āśrava* leads to *bandha* or the bondage of the self. On account of *yoga*, *karmas* begin to collect in the self, bringing about its bondage. It is to be noted that along with the inflow of *karmas* into the self, passions or *kaṣāyas* make their appearance and as a consequence of that, the self goes along the path of its own bondage[2]. And by continuing to take in the *karma* matter, there arises in it *mithyātva* or false faith, *avirati* or non-restraint and *pramāda* or delusion. And, these are the causes of the bondage of the self (*bandha-hetavaḥ*).

1. *kāyavāṅmanaḥkarmayogaḥ sa āśravaḥ*, *TS*, VII. 12.

2. *sakaṣāyatvājjīvaḥ karmaṇo yogyān pudgalānādatte, sa bandhah*, *ibid.*, VIII. 2-3.

(5) *Saṁvara*—*Saṁvara* may be called stopping the inflow of *karma* matter. The inflow of the *karmic* matter may be stopped and this is called *saṁvara*[1]. The self, that wants salvation, must first try to break the fetters of *karma*. Ordinarily it is very difficult to break them off, all of a sudden, because the activities of the self are first directed to the stoppage of the *karma*-flow or *āśrava*. *Saṁvara* consists in the stoppage of the *āśrava*. It prevents the further inflow of *karma*. It is brought about by the threefold restraint of body, mind and speech (*kāyagupti*, *manogupti*, *vacanagupti*), and by the performance of duties (*samiti*), by pity towards all living beings (*dharma*), by the suffering of privations (*pariṣahajaya*), by penance (*tapasā*), by contemplation of the unsatisfactory nature of the world (*anutprekṣā*) and by good conduct (*cāritra*)[2] for the achievement thereof.

(6) *Nirjarā*—*Nirjarā* means the falling away of the *karmic* matters from the self. *Saṁvara* stops the inflow of fresh *karmas*. But it is also necessary that the already collected *karmas* should be destroyed, because salvation is impossible so long as *karmas* remain in the self. *Nirjarā* consists in the annihilation of the already introduced *karmas*. It is of two types—*savipāka* and *avipāka*. The former consists in the annihilation of the *karmas*, which arise when their fruits are all enjoyed. *Avipāka nirjarā* is the destruction of the *karmas* through penance etc., even before their fruits have been enjoyed.

(7) *Mokṣa*—It may be called liberation from *karma* or complete freedom of the self from *karmic* matter. When *āśrava* is stopped, *bandha* becomes loosened, the already collected *karmas* are destroyed by *nirjarā* and thus the *karmas* disappear from the self altogether. In the state of salvation there is no bondage. *Mokṣa* consists in the state of infinite knowledge, infinite vision, infinite power and infinite joy (*anantajñāna*,

1. *āśravanirodhaḥ saṁvaraḥ*, *TS*, IX. 1.
2. *Ibid.* IX.2.

anantadarśana, *anantavīrya* and *anantānanda*) in the self. The self returns to its natural state. Thus, the *karmic* matters are the cause of ignorance or the obstructions of knowledge. There are eight types of *karmic* matters —one of them is the *jñānāvaraṇīya karma* or the knowledge obscuring matter[1]. The *jñānāvarṇīya karma* or the knowledge obscuring *karmas* is sub-divided into five types. This classification is based on the classification of knowledge[2]. In the Jaina *Āgamas*, knowledge is described as being of five types—*ābhinibodhika* or *matijñāna*, *śrutajñāna*, *avadhijñāna*, *manaḥparyāyajñāna* and *kevalajñāna*. There are also five corresponding knowledge-obscuring *karmas*—*matijñānāvaraṇīya*, *śrutajñānāvaraṇīya*, *avadhijñānāvaraṇīya*, *manaḥparyāyajñānāvaraṇīya* and the *kevalajñānāvaraṇīya*. Due to these five types of *āvaraṇas*, the five types of knowledge are obscured or not manifested. When an *āvaraṇa* is destroyed the knowledge which it concealed is manifested. The first four types of knowledge are partial knowledges and the last alone is the perfect or infinite knowledge.

2. *Relation Between Self and Karmas*

The matter or the *pudgalas* which attract the self are very subtle and cannot be seen by an eye or even by any instrument; only an omniscient being may perceive them[3]. They belong to the whole atmosphere and due to the activities of body, mind and speech they are attracted towards the self.

The relation of the self and matter has existed from time immemorial. Matter mixes with the self just as water mixes with milk; the relation between the self and matter is called as a relation of water and milk[4]. There is a link of the relation; the old matters of the self affect its present activity and the present activities determine the future of the self[5]. But

1. *Karmagrantha* I, p. 8.
2. *Ibid.*, I, p. 9.
3. *Ibid.*, I, p. 2.
4. *Ibid.*
5. *Ibid.*

the relation of the self and matter is not permanent[1]. When the self possesses the *bhedajñāna* or *viveka*, that is, the self realises that the matter and the self are different, the self is pure, but due to its relation with matter it cannot exist in its natural state. As soon as the self realises the difference, it tries to search for the causes of the relation and tries to avoid the causes. In scriptures, the passions (*kaṣāyas*) are said to be the causes; the *rāgādi* are the causes or *hetu* of the bondage of the self. Therefore, when the self realises the difference between the self and matter it tries to give up passions with the help of mental and bodily discipline and meditation. And gradually it becomes successful; it becomes pure. Then no more the relation, and so the self comes to its natural stage; it becomes pure and perfect and there arises infinite knowledge. This pure self may be called *Jina*, *Arhat* or *Paramātmā*.

The question may be asked, if knowledge is the essential quality of the self then how it is veiled by the *karmic* matters ? Hemacandra would reply[2] that though the self is obscured by the veil of the *karmic* matters, yet there is no harm to the nature of the self; the light of knowledge is not destroyed by the veil in the same way as the light of the sun or moon is not destroyed by the veil of the clouds. The obstructions of the *karmic* matter upon the self is beginningless, but it ends, just as gold has dust and other substances, but they may be removed by some materials and then gold can be made pure. In the same way, the veil of the *karmic* matter may be destroyed or removed by the regular practices of bodily and mental discipline and meditation.

Again, it may be asked, if the self is formless then how could it be obscured by matter ? The reply would be thus : though consciousness has no form, yet it is found to be influenced by wine etc. In the same way the formless self may be influenced by the *karmas*[3].

Another question may be asked, is the nature of the self changed by the obstruction of the *karmas* ? Since self is eternal, how can it be influenced by the *karmas* ? The Jainas reply that the self is eternal in one sense and non-eternal in another

1. *Karmagrantha*, I, p. 3.
2. *PM*, I. 1.15.
3. *Ibid.*

sense. Self is eternal in its essential nature; the *karmic* matters do not influence its essential nature. But the self is non-eternal in the sense that its attribute or the *paryāyas* are changing, they come and go; they have beginning and end; they are not eternal. Thus, the self is not *kūṭasthanitya* but *pariṇāminitya*. That is why, though eternal, yet it undergoes change[1].

3. *The Meaning of the Mukhya Pratyakṣa*

As mentioned before, *mukhya pratyakṣa* is the direct knowledge, which arises in the self directly without the help of the sense-organs and mind. It arises when the obstruction of the *karmas* is destroyed. The word *mukhya* means superior, therefore *mukhya pratyakṣa* is defined as superior knowledge. As the face has a superior status compared to the other parts of the body, *mukhya pratyakṣa* is also superior amongst all knowledges. The Jainas believe that *mukhya pratyakṣa* is of three types—*avadhi*, *manaḥaparyāya*, *kevala*. These are the direct knowledges by the self itself and are not based on the instrumentality of the sense-organs and the mind. The *kevala* or omniscience occurs when there is complete destruction of all *karmas*. But when the destruction of the veil is not complete, the two other varieties, the *avadhi* and the *manaḥparyāya*, appear[2].

4. *The Definition of Mukhya Pratyakṣa*

In the *Āgamika* literature, *mukhya pratyakṣa* only is called simply as *pratyakṣa* ; *pratyakṣa* is there defined as the direct knowledge in the sense that it arises in the self without the help of the sense organs and mind. But later on in the logical literature *pratyakṣa* is classified into two types—the *sāṁvyavahārika* and the *mukhya*.

The *mukhya pratyakṣa* is defined in different ways by different Jaina philosophers, although the meanings are not very different. For example, Akalaṅka defines it thus[3] : "the *mukhya pratyakṣa* is not caused by sense-organs, it arises in the

1. *PM*, 1. 1. 15

2. *tat sarvathāvaraṇavilaye cetanasya svarūpāvirbhāve mukhyaṁ kevalaṁ, tattāratamye'vadhimanaḥparyāyau, ca, ibid.*, I. 1.15, 18.

3. *mukhyam atīndriyam jñānam, AGT*, p. 2.

self". Vādideva defines it thus : "the *pārmārthika pratyakṣa* arises in the self without any intermediation."[1] Māṇikyanandi and Hemacandra also define it as a perfect knowledge arising in the self without the instrumentality of the sense-organs. Now we will try to explain Māṇikyanandi's definition of the *mukhya pratyakṣa*.

Māṇikyanandi defines *mukhya pratyakṣa* thus : "*Mukhya* is that clear, non-sensuous and infinite knowledge of which all veils are removed by special conditions[2]". The question may be asked as to what is the speciality of such infinite knowledge. The commentator Prabhācandra replies that it arises when all the veils of the *karmas* are removed completely under special conditions (*sāmagrīviśeṣa*). Right faith (*samyakdarśana*), is the internal condition while space, time etc. are the external conditions. When all these conditions are favourable, the *karmas* are removed completely and there arises the *mukhya pratyakṣa*.

Prabhācandra explains *mukhya pratyakṣa* with the help of an inference : "wherever there is clear and true knowledge, there is the destruction of all veils, just as in the case of perception of trees etc. which were being enclosed by clouds or mist[3]". *Mukhya pratyakṣa* is clear and right knowledge. It is non-sensuous (*atīndriya*), i.e., does not depend on mind and the sense-organs, so it is perfect and infinite. Whatever is not non-sensuous does not possess the adjective "is independent of the mind and the senses" (*yattu nātindriyādisvabhāvaṁ na tattadanapekṣatvādiviśeṣaṇaviśiṣṭam*), just as our ordinary sensuous knowledge, which is caused by the sense-organs and the mind. Thus, the *mukhya* is that *pratyakṣa* which is non-sensuous, infinite; whatever is not of this kind, is not *mukhya*, just as our sensuous knowledge.

The Buddhists may point out that it is not true that knowledge arises by the destruction of the obstruction of knowledge (*Jñānāvaraṇa*). There are no such obstructions (*āvaraṇas*). If there were such a veil then what is that obstruction ? Is it the body or the passions (*rāgādi*) or the time, space etc. ? The

1. *pāramārthikaṁ punarutpattāvātmamātrāpekṣam, PNT,* II. 18.

2. *sāmagrīviśeṣaviśleṣitākhilāvaraṇamatīndriyaṁ aśeṣato mukhyaṁ PKM,* p. 241.

3. *yadyatra spaṣṭatve satyavitathaṁ jñānaṁ tat tatrāpagatākhilāvaraṇaṁ yathā rajonīhārādyantaritavṛkṣādau tadapagamaprabhovaṁ jñānam, ibid.*

body and the passions are not the obstructions of knowledge, for knowledge is found to arise even in their presence. The Jainas may reply that the existence of obstructions of knowledge (*jñānāvaraṇas*) is well known. Prabhācandra tries to prove the existence of *āvaraṇa* with the help of an inference. "Whatever knowledge does not apprehend its own object, is a *sāvaraṇa*; just as the defective eye cannot apprehend its own object, i.e., the one moon and perceives two moons. Knowledge can intrinsically apprehend all objects; it is infinite but it cannot, in fact, know all objects. Therefore, its limitations must be due to some *āvaraṇa*[1].

The *Advaitins* hold that *avidyā* is the *āvaraṇa*, not the *karmic* matter, because something (*mūrta*) cannot veil the immaterial (*amūrta*) knowledge. For if it were so, then the body may also be the *āvaraṇa*. The Jainas point out that this is not true, because it is found that intoxicants which are material may obscure knowledge. There is no such rule that the *āvaraṇa* of knowledge must be itself immaterial[2].

According to the *Yoga*, *karma* is a quality of the self, it is not a *pudgala*. The Jainas point out that if the *karmas* are the quality of the self then they could not be the cause of bondage of the self. And in that case, either the self should be completely in bondage or always free. Whatever is the quality of something cannot be the cause of the bondage of that thing, just as colour etc. are the quality of earth but not the cause of its bondage. Therefore, *karmas* are also not the quality of the self, for they are the cause of its bondage.

The *Sāṁkhyas* hold that the *karmas* are not the quality of the self but they are the production of *prakṛti*. The Jainas would reject this for they do not believe in the *Sāṁkhya* theory of *prakṛti*. A question may be asked, if there are *karmas* and if the chain of *karmas* be beginningless, then how is the obstruction of the *karmas* to be destroyed? The Jainas reply that there are some special conditions under which they may be destroyed; these are the right knowledge (*samyakjñāna*), right faith (*samyakdarśana*), and right conduct (*samyakcāritrya*). These three

1. *yad jñānaṁ svaviṣaye'pravṛttimat tat sāvaraṇaṁ yathā kāmalino locanavijñānamekacandramasi, svaviṣaye aśeṣārthalakṣaṇe'pravṛttimacca jñānamiti*, *ibid.* p. 242.

2. *madirādinā mūrtenāpyamurtasya jñānāderāvaraṇadarśanāt*, *ibid.*, p. 243.

are the ways by which the *karmas* are destroyed. Prabhācandra holds that there are *nirjarā* and *saṁvara* which make the self free from the obstruction of the *karmas*. The possibility of *nirjarā* may be proved by the following inference; "the *karmas* of the self may sometimes be all destroyed because their effects are exhausted. If something is not destroyed then its power of producing effects does not come to an end, as in the case of time".

Again, there is the principle of *saṁvara*. *Saṁvara* stops the *karma* attraction towards the self. Thus Prabhācandra says that *nirjarā* and *saṁvara* destroy the beginningless *karma* obstruction of the self[1].

5. *Kinds of Mukhya Pratyakṣa*

The Jainas hold that there are three types of *mukhya pratyakṣa*-*avadhijñāna*, *manaḥparyāyajñāna* and *kevalajñāna*. The former two are called as *deśapratyakṣa* and the last one called *sarvapratyakṣa*[2] (or *vikalapratyakṣa* and *sakalapratyakṣa*). Although all the three types of *mukhya pratyakṣa* are nonsensuous and they all arise in the self directly, yet the *deśapratyakṣa* are partial knowledges. The *sarvapratyakṣa* is the knowledge of all; it is perfect and infinite knowledge. Thus the *kevalajñāna* is the knowledge of all, it is omniscience. The three types of *mukhyapratyakṣa* may now be explained one by one.

Avadhi Jñāna :

As mentioned before, there are five types of knowledge according to the Jaina *Āgamas*—namely, *mati*, *śruta*, *avadhi*, *manaḥparyāya* and *kevala*. The former two are sensuous knowledge and are called *sāṁvyavahārika pratyakṣa* and the latter three are non-sensuous knowledge and are called *mukhya pratyakṣa* in the logical literature. The Jainas hold that the self possesses infinite knowledge as its essential quality but due to the obstruction of the *karmas* this infinite knowledge is not manifested. When the obstructions are destroyed, the knowledge arises.

1. All the arguments are quoted from *PKM*, pp. 241-46.
2. *tad dvedhā deśapratyakṣaṁ sarvapratyakṣaṁ ca deśapratyakṣamavadhimanaḥparyāyajñāne, sarvapratyakṣaṁ kevalam*, *IV*, I. 20.15.

There are five types of obstruction corresponding to the five types of knowledge. Each type of knowledge is obscured by its own obstruction or *jñānāvaraṇa*[1]. As for example, *matijñāna* is obscured by *matijñānāvaraṇa* and it arises by destruction and subsidence (*kṣayopaśama*) of its *karmic* veil (*matijñānāvaraṇa*). In the same way, *avadhijñāna* arises by the destruction and subsidence of the *avadhijñānāvaraṇa*.

The *avadhijñāna* is non-sensuous knowledge. It arises in the self without the help of the sense-organs and the mind. *Avadhi* means limitation, though *avadhijñāna* is non-sensuous yet it is limited, because due to *avadhi* one can perceive the objects which possess form or shape (*rūpin*)[2]. All the objects which have form are manifested in *avadhi* but all their modes cannot be manifested in this knowledge. It apprehends the objects which possess form, although the objects are of the past, future or are distant. It can apprehend very fine objects, such as the atoms and the *karmic* matter etc. All these objects are known by the self directly.

Avadhijñāna is divided into many types. All kinds of *avadhijñāna* cannot apprehend all objects of all space and of all time. This faculty differs in different beings on account of the development of their spiritual discipline. The highest type of *avadhijñāna* is able to apprehend the material objects of all time and of all space. The lower type of *avadhijñāna* extends to a very small fraction of space and time[3].

The question may arise as to who possesses this knowledge. With respect to its possessor, the *avadhijñāna* is of two types[4] — *bhavapratyaya* and *guṇapratyaya*. The former is that which arises in a person due to his birth; for example, the beings of heaven and hell acquire this kind of *avadhijñāna* which is their birth right[5]. The *guṇapratyaya avadhijñāna* is that which has to be acquired as a result of special merit. Everybody can acquire it when his *avadhijñānāvaraṇa* is destroyed by meditation and discipline. Although both types of *avadhijñāna* arise by destruction and subsidence of its *karmika* veils, yet for the

1. *Karmagrantha* I, p. 9.
2. *rūpiṣvavadheḥ*, *TS*, I. 28.
3. For various types of *avadhijñāna* see *Nandisūtra*, 16 and *TV*, I. 21-22.
4. *dvividhaḥ avadhiḥ*, *TS*, I. 21.
5. *Ibid.*, I. 22.

bhavapratyaya-avadhijñāna the *nimitta kāraṇa* is the birth of the beings who possess it. Just as the birds acquire the capacity of flying in the sky from their very birth, similarly the beings of heaven and hell acquire *avadhijñāna* from their birth.[1] This *avadhijñāna* is not the highest type of *avadhijñāna*; it is a limited *avadhijñāna*.

Manaḥparyāya Jñāna :

Mind, according to the Jainas is a material substance. Its modes are its different changing states. As our states of thought change, the modes also change correspondingly. These changing modes of mind are called *manaḥparyāya*. And the knowledge which knows the modes of thinking of the mind of other persons is called *manaḥparyāyajñāna*[2]. A person possessing *manaḥparyāyajñāna* directly knows the others' mental states without the help of sense organs and mind. Such knowledge arises by the destruction and subsidence of *manaḥparyāya jñānāvaraṇa*[3].

There are different views regarding the nature of *manaḥparyāyajñāna*[4]. According to Jinabhadra, in the *manaḥparyāyajñāna*, one perceives the states of the mindsubstance directly, but the external objects of thoughts of another mind are known only by inference, because the external objects of thought may be material or non-material (*mūrta* or *amūrta*) and the non-material objects cannot be apprehended directly by *manaḥparyāyajñāna*. (The *amūrta* are known directly only in *kevala*). Thus, according to this view, only the modes of mind are directly cognised in *manaḥparyāyajñāna*.

Akalaṅka rejects this and points out that *manaḥparyāya jñāna* also apprehends directly the objects of others' thoughts. The knowledge of such objects cannot be an inference, it is perceptual knowledge. It possesses the characteristics of *pratyakṣa*; it is clear and it is direct and not dependent on sense organs and mind. Therefore, it should not be regarded as an inference, which is not clear and independent[5]. Akalaṅka holds that the external objects also are directly apprehended by

1. *TS*. I. 22.
2. *parakīyamanogatārthajñānaṁ manaḥparyāyaḥ*, IV. I. 9.4.
3. *tadāvaraṇakarmakṣayopaśamādidvitayanimittavaśāt parakīyamanogatārthajñānaṁ manaḥparyāyaḥ*, *ibid*. 4.
4. TATIYA, N. M., *Studies in Jaina Philosophy*, p. 66.
5. *TV*, I. 23. 4.

manaḥparyāyajñāna, as they are associated with the mind which is thinking of them.

According to Hemacandra, the external objects of others' mind are not apprehended directly in *manaḥparyāyajñāna*; they are known only by inference[1].

Further, *manaḥparyāyajñāna* should not be understood as a knowledge derived from mind; it is not any type of mental perception. But it is a non-sensuous knowledge arising within the self directly, without the help of sense-organs or mind. Mind is not the cause of this knowledge, but it is the knowledge of the mental states of others, which is derived from the self itself. Thus, it is not empirical knowledge. Akalaṅka argues that mind is only the *apekṣā* in this knowledge, not the cause. For example, when one sees the moon in the sky he cannot see the moon without perceiving the sky. The sky is only the *apekṣā* in the knowledge of the moon, not its cause. In the same way mind is not the cause in *manaḥparyāyajñāna* but only an *apekṣā* or a factor depending on which one perceives the mental states of others[2].

Manaḥparyāyajñāna is of two types—namely *ṛjumati* and *vipulamati*. In respect of purity and duration, they are different[3]. *Ṛjumati* is less pure and it sometimes falters. *Vipulamati* is purer, clearer and more enduring. It lasts up to the rise of omniscience. Man can possess both types of *manaḥparyāyajñāna* in the state of spiritual perfection.

Kevalajñāna :

Kevalajñāna is the perfect and infinite knowledge. We may call it omniscience. As mentioned before, when the obstructions of all the *karmas* are destroyed, the self attains *kevala* or omniscience. In this knowledge one apprehends simultaneously all substances and all their qualities directly without the help of sense-organs and mind. Nothing remains to be known and nothing is unknown[4]. It is perfect and eternal knowledge. The causes of omniscience are two internal and external. Internal

1. *manaḥparyāyā anyathānupapattyā tu yad bāhya-cintanīyā arthajñānaṁ tat ānumānikameva na manaḥparyāya-pratyakṣam*, *PM*, I. 1. 18.
2. *TV*, 1. 23. 2.
3. *TS* and *TB*, 1. 24, 25.
4. *Ibid.*, I. 30.

causes are right faith etc. and the external causes are time, space etc. According to the Jainas, there would-be possessor of omniscience should have his births as a human being within the specified time. Omniscience arises from the destruction of all the *karmas*. A question frequently discussed is whether the four imperfect knowledges (*mati, śruta, avadhi* and *manaḥ-paryāya*) are present or not, in the state of omniscience. Some hold that in the state of *kevalajñāna* the other four knowledges exist, but they are overpowered by the *kevalajñāna*, just as in the daytime the light of the stars is overpowered by the light of the sun. Umāsvāti points out that this view is not true, because the *kevala* arises due to the total destruction (*kṣaya*) of all *karmic* matters, while the other four knowledges arise by the destruction and subsidence (*Kṣayopaśama*) of their own *jñānā-varaṇas* or the *karmic* matters. When there is the total destruction of *karmic* matters the other knowledges also could not arise. There would be only the state of omniscience[1].

Yaśovijaya holds in this connection that there are five types of knowledge as well as five types of *āvaraṇa*. In other words, a particular *jñāna* has its own *āvaraṇa* as an obstruction to its manifestation, and when its *āvaraṇa* is destroyed, that knowledge is manifested. When the *āvaraṇa* of the perfect knowledge (*kevalajñānāvaraṇa*) is destroyed then arises perfect knowledge of the *kevalajñāna*. The main question is when the *āvaraṇa* of *kevalajñāna* is destroyed and one possesses perfect or infinite knowledge, then does he also possess the other partial knowledges or not? The partial knowledges arise due to the destruction of their own different *āvaraṇas*. Yaśovijaya replies that though the different knowledges are manifested by the destruction of their own knowledge-obscuring *karmas*, yet the *āvaraṇa* of perfect knowledge is also at the same time the cause of the manifestation of imperfect knowledge, just as the veil of a cloth may be both an obstruction of clear vision and also a cause of unclear vision[2]. In other words the obstruction of perfect knowledge is the cause of the manifestation of imperfect knowledge. Thus, according to Yaśovijaya, for an omniscient person, partial knowledge is not possible, for the cause of partial knowledge,

1. *TB*, I. 31.

2. *spaṣṭaprakāśapratibandhako mandaprakāśajanakatvam anutkaṭe cakṣurādyā-varaṇe vastrādeva*, *JBP*. 4.

i.e., the *kevalajñānāvaraṇīya*, has been destroyed[1]. It may be asked, how can the self be both *āvṛta* and *anāvṛt* at one and the same time? In reply, it is said that this is possible only from the *anekānta* viewpoint. The self may be obscured by the *kevala-jñānāvaraṇa*, and the same self may not be obscured by the *mati-jñānāvaraṇa* at the same time. Yaśovijaya says that knowledge is the essential quality of the self but it has many modes (*paryāya*). These modes are the partial knowledges, and when the perfect knowledge is *āvṛta* by the *kevalajñānāvaraṇa* the partial knowledges may be *anāvṛta*. And as the knowledge is the essential quality of the self, the self would be both *āvṛta* and *anāvṛta* by the obstruction of different kinds of *karmas* at one and the same time.

Kundakunda's Explanation of Kevalajñāna :

Kundakunda explains the nature of *kevalajñāna* with the help of *niścaya dṛṣṭi* and *vyavahāra dṛṣṭi*. Therefore, it will be necessary to understand at first what is the *niścaya dṛṣṭi* and what is the *vyavahāra dṛṣṭi*.

The words *niścaya* and *vyavahāra* are used in the Jaina philosophy in different senses. But generally they are used as the names of two different points of view, because the Jainas explain a thing from different points of view. Thus, *niścaya dṛṣṭi* and *vyavahāra dṛṣṭi* are the two different points of view from which the nature of a thing may be explained. Sometimes the *niścaya dṛṣṭi* is also called *paramārtha dṛṣṭi* and the *vyavahāra dṛṣṭi* is called *saṁvṛta-dṛṣṭi*. With the help of the *niścaya dṛṣṭi*, one knows the essential nature or the *ābhyantarasvarūpa* of a thing, and with the help of *vyavahāra dṛṣṭi* one knows the secondary properties or the *bāhya sarūpa* of a thing.

Kundakunda explains the nature of *kevalajñāna* from these two different viewpoints. According to *niścaya dṛṣṭi*, *kevalajñāna* is self-revealing, a *kevalī* is indifferent to the world, so he knows or sees only his pure self. In other words, in the state of *kevala-jñāna* one has the intuitive experience of his own pure self. But according to *vyavahāra dṛṣṭi*, he knows also the objects of all time and place.

Since knowledge is the essential quality of the self, it is self-revealing; if knowledge does not know itself then it would not

1. *tatra hetuḥ kevalajñānāvaraṇameva*, *ibid.* 3.

be the essential quality of the self[1]. Knowledge is also object-revealing. Kundakunda gives two characteristics of knowledge from two different points of view. From one view point, knowledge is self-revealing, (i.e., from the *niścaya dṛṣṭi*) and from the other, knowledge is object-revealing (i.e., from the *vyavahāra dṛṣṭi*). Thus, the nature of knowledge is explained by him as being both self-revealing and object-revealing. Again he says that the *kevalajñānī* or the possessor of *kevalajñāna*, sees or knows all things only from the *vyavahāra dṛṣṭi*, but from the *niścaya dṛṣṭi*, he knows only the self itself[2].

In the next *Sūtra* Kundakunda explains that the *kevalajñānī* is indifferent to the world and so although he perceives all things his mind is not attracted to them and he may be said not to know them. His self becomes pure, so he possesses the intuitional experience of the self itself; therefore, he is called *abandhaka*[3]. The commentator says that the Jinendra knows all the objects of all time but he is indifferent to all; he only apprehends, his own self[4].

Further, Kundakunda says that the *kevalī* sees his own nature, not the world[5]. Here the commentator explains that from the view point of niścaya,[6] the *kevali* being wholly directed

1. *ṇāṇaṁ jīvasarūpaṁ tamhā jaṇei appagaṁ appā, appāṇaṁ ṇavi jāṇadi appādo hodi vidirittaṁ,*

jñānaṁ jīvasvarūpaṁ tasmājjānātyātmakam ātmā, ātmānaṁ nāpi jānātyātmano bhavati vyatiriktaṁ-tātparyavṛtti on Niyamasāra, 169.

2. *jāṇadi passadi savvaṁ vavahāraṇayeṇa kevalī bhagavaṁ, kevalaṇāṇī jāṇadi passadi ṇiyameṇa appāṇaṁ, (jānāti paśyati sarvaṁ vyavahāranayena kevalī bhagavān, kevalajñānī jānāti paśyati niyamena ātmānam) ibid.* 158.

3. *jāṅto passaṅto Ihāpuvvam ṇa hoi kevaliṇo, kevaliṇāṇī tamhā teṇa du so'bandhago bhaṇido, (jānan paśyannīhāpurvvaṁ na bhavati kevalinaḥ, kevalajñānī tasmāt tena tu śobandhako bhaṇitaḥ), ibid.* 171.

4. *jānan sarvaṁ bhuvanabhavanābhyantarasthaṁ padārthaṁ, paśyan tadvat sahajamahimā devadevo jineśaḥ, mohābhāvātparamamakhilaṁ naiva gṛhṇāti nityaṁ, jñānajyotirhatamalakaliḥ sarvalokaikasākṣī, ibid.* 171.

5. *appasarūpaṁ pecchadi loyāloyaṁ ṇa kevalī bhagavaṁ—Niyamasāra*, 165; (*ātmasvarūpaṁ paśyati lokālokau na kevalī bhagavān—Tātparyavṛtti*, 165).

6. *paramanirapekṣatayā niḥśeṣato'ntarmukhatvāt kevalasvarūpa-pratyakṣamātra—vyāpāro-niratanirañjananijasahajadarśanena saccidānandamayamātmānaṁ niścayataḥ paśyatīti, paśyatyātmā sahajaparamātmānamekaṁ viśudhaṁ svāntaḥ śudhyāvasathamahimādhāramatyantadhīram, ibid.*

inwards and being completely indifferent to outward objects, knows only his own self by a sort of intuition.

After describing the nature of *kevalajñāna* from the *niścaya dṛṣṭi*, he explains it next from the *vyavahāra dṛṣṭi*. From this point of view, the *kevalī* knows the whole world, not his pure self[1].

Thus *kevalajñāna* is self-revealing and also object-revealing, from two different points of view. But the essential nature of *kevalajñāna* is to be self revealing, there is the intuitive experience of the pure self. Because knowledge is the essential quality of the self. When all the *āvaraṇas* are destroyed the self is manifes ted in its own nature.

6. *The Jaina View of Non-Sensuous Perception*

We have explained the different kinds of non-sensuous perception recognised in the different schools of Indian philosophy. In the *Nyāya* system, there are three types of extra-ordinary perceptions. Of these, the first two—*sāmānyalakṣaṇa* and *jñānalakṣaṇa*—cannot be called *atīndriyapratyakṣa* or non-sensuous perception from the Jaina point of view. *Atīndriya pratyakṣa* is a perception which is not caused by the sense-organs and mind, while *sāmānyalakṣaṇa* and *jñānalakṣaṇa* arise with the help of the senses. Though there is no direct sense-object contact, yet there is indirect or extraordinary sense-object contact. Therefore, according to the Jainas, these cannot be called *alaukika* or *atīndriya pratyakṣa*. The Jainas may point out that *sāmānyalakṣaṇa* is not a perception at all, for *pratyakṣa*, according to the Jainas, is a clear (*viśada*) knowledge, but the so-called *sāmānyalakṣaṇa* perception of all members of a class is not *viśada* or direct knowledge and so is not perception.

As regards *jñānalakṣaṇa* the Jainas point out that it is a mixed mode of knowledge (*samūhālambana jñāna*) in which the visual perception of sandal and idea of fragrance are integrated into one knowledge[2]. Thus, it is not the *atīndriya pratyakṣa*.

The *Yogī pratyakṣa* of the *Naiyāyikas* may be called as *alaukika pratyakṣa* or the *atīndriya pratyakṣa*, for it is not caused by the

1. *loyāloyaṁ jāṇai appāṇaṁ naiva kevalī bhagavaṁ*—*Niyamasāra*. 168, (*lokālokau jānātyātmānaṁ naiva kevalī bhagavān*—*Tātparyavṛtti* 168).

2. Radhakrishnan, S., *Indian Philosophy*, II, p. 60.

sense-organs; it is the direct apprehension of the objects of the past, future and distance. It may be compared with the *kevala jñāna* of the Jainas.

Again, the *Brahmānubhava* of the *Advaitins* is *atīndriya jñāna* but there is no knowledge of the objects of the past, future and distance, just as in the *Yogī pratyakṣa* or in the *kevala jñāna*. According to the *Advaitins*, the world is not real but only appears as real due to ignorance. There is only one reality, that is, Brahman, so that there is no question of a direct apprehension of all the objects of all the world in the *Brahmajñāna*. There is the direct apprehension only of the self itself, which is called *Brahman*. The Jainas also believe in the direct apprehension of the pure self in the stage of *kevala*, because, according to them, in that stage all *āvaraṇas* are destroyed and the self becomes pure, and it is called *Jina*, *Arhata* or *Paramātmā*. The Jaina experience of the pure self may be compared with the *Brahmānubhava*. The difference between *Brahmajñāna* and *kevalajñāna* seems to be that, since the Jainas believe in the reality of the external world, therefore, in their *kevalajñāna* there is the direct apprehension of external objects of all time and all place. But so far as the experience of the self itself is concerned, the difference between *Brahmajñāna* and *kevalajñāna* is not so great. There is truly some difference between the experience of the self in the two systems. According to the *Advaitins*, there is only one self (Brahman) so that in the *Brahmajñāna* the individual self possesses the experience of identity with Brahman (*I am Brahman*). But in the *kevalajñāna* different selves have the pure feeling of their own existence for all selves and are different.

Further, the *Yoga* system believes that a *Yogī* can acquire supernormal powers in a particular state of *Yoga sādhanā*. He may acquire omniscience. The Jainas would agree with this. They hold that by the practice of mental and bodily discipline, when all the *āvaraṇas* are destroyed, man can acquire some special qualities. Hemacandra says that due to the destruction and subsidence of the *karmic* matters they possess different types of special qualities, but they are indifferent to them, because their only desire is to get release.

The *Yogī-pratyakṣa* of the Buddhists may be called as *atīndriya pratyakṣa*, because it is not caused by sense-organs; it is the direct intuition of transcendental reality. But the Jainas do not accept the *nirvikalpa* character of it. For, according to the Jainas, true knowledge must be determinate or *savikalpa*. As mentioned before, determinateness is the criterion of right knowledge. If it is not determinate it cannot contradict error, doubt, etc.[1].

7. *Kumāril's objections and the Jaina arguments for the possibility of the omniscient being*

(a) *The Arguments of Prabhācandra*[2] :

As mentioned before, the Jaina theory of knowledge is based on their conception of self. Self is omniscient, but due to the veil of the *karmic* matters this knowledge is obscured. This obstruction can be removed totally by the practice of mental discipline and meditation, just as the clouds which conceal the sun or the moon can be removed by a blast of wind. And when all the obstructions are removed the self gains omniscience.

Kumārila does not accept this view of omniscience. According to him, the self is not able to know directly all objects of all time. He argues that the knowledge of the past, present and future is attained only through the *Vedas* which are authorless (*apauruṣeya*). There is no such person who attains the faculty of such knowledge through direct perception. Thus, there can be no omniscience and there is no *pramāṇa* to prove the existence of any omniscient being. The Jainas reject this view that there is no *pramāṇa* to prove the existence of the omniscient person. They maintain that one can prove it by inferences. One of the inferences used by the Jainas is as follows : there is a person who perceives all objects; for it is his nature to know all things and also the obstructions for such knowledge have been destroyed. If a thing by its very nature can know other thing, and the obstructions which hinder such knowledge have been destroyed, then it should be able to perceive such thing. For example, it is the nature of the eyes to perceive colour and if there is no darkness, then the eyes would perceive colour. The Jainas hold that there is perceptual knowledge of objects which

1. *PKM.*, p. 27.
2. All arguments are taken from *PKM* pp. 247-65.

are subtle or which are too far or which are past, because they are *prameyas* just as fire. The *Mīmāṁsakas* reject this and ask; are all these objects apprehended by one perception or is each object apprehended by a different perception? In the first case, *hetu* would be *viruddha* for *prameyattva* is known to belong only to such objects each of which is apprehended by a different perception. If one perception apprehends all objects, then this totality would not be a *prameya*. In the second case, there is also the fallacy of *siddhasādhana* for even the *Mīmāṁsakas* would accept it.

The Jainas do not accept that the omniscient person apprehends each object in a different perception; what they believe is that the objects—far away objects of past and the subtle objects etc.—are apprehended by perception[1] in general (*pratyakṣasāmānyena*). Further, whatever is apprehended by omniscience is not caused by sense-organs and mind, as in the case of *Yogī pratyakṣa*. These two propositions together prove that there is a non-sensuous direct knowledge of allt hings, omniscient beings, perception being one or many.

Again, the *Mīmāṁsakas* ask, is omniscience the knowledge of all things or of some very important things only? If it is the knowledge of all things, does it arise gradually or simultaneously? If it arises gradually then the knowledge of the past, present, future, distant and infinite would be impossible. It cannot arise simultaneously for there are opposite natures of different things (just as water is cold and fire is hot). And perceptions of all such different things cannot arise simultaneously in one knowledge.

Prabhācandra asks, why cannot objects of opposed nature be apprehended simultaneously in one knowledge? Is it because of the absence of such objects or because knowledge is unable to apprehend them simultaneously? The first alternative is not true, for things with opposed characters are well known to exist simultaneously as in a piece of wood, which may be warm in one part and cold in another. The second alternative is also not true, because knowledge is known to apprehend opposite things simultaneously; for example, it

1. *pratyakṣasāmānyena kasyacitsūkṣmādyarthānāṁ pratyakṣatvasādhanāt, ibid.*, p. 256.

is well-known that light and darkness may be apprehended in the same knowledge together. The *mīmāṁsakas* may further argue that the past and the future cannot be known in omniscience because they are not present. The absent things cannot be apprehended; the knowledge of absent things would be as false as a perception by a defective sense organ. But if such objects are present then why are they called past or future? If an object of one time is apprehended as belonging to another time (e.g., if the past and the future are apprehended as being present) then such knowledge would be invalid.

The Jainas reject this argument. They point out that the knowledge of the past and future is possible in omniscience, because the objects of the past are apprehended as of the past and the objects of future are apprehended as of the future. There is no question of the absence of the objects of the past and of the future, for all objects of all times are apprehended in omniscience as belonging to their own times[1].

(b) *The Arguments of Hemacandra*

The critics may argue that perception cannot prove it because perception gives us knowledge only of sensible qualities; it cannot give us knowledge of what is supersensible. Omniscience cannot be proved by inference also, because the process of an inference depends on the relation between *sādhya* and *hetu*, both of which must be perceived. Inference is based on previous knowledge which is derived from sense experience. But in the case of omniscience there is no such knowledge from sense experience; therefore it cannot be proved by inference. It cannot be proved by verbal testimony also for verbal knowledge is also based on sense perception. Therefore, the existence of omniscience cannot be proved.

To all these objections against the possibility of omniscience Hemacandra gives the following reply[2]. He points out that if knowledge has a process in its development then there must be an end of this process. At this end it must be fully developed and it is the stage where knowledge could be called perfect or infinite and that is omniscience. Again, the knowledge of the objects, which are far and which are fine is possible. Fine

1. *svakālaniyatasattvarūpatayaiva tasya grahaṇāt, ibid.*, p. 261.
2. *kasyacit pratyakṣāḥ prameyatvād ghaṭavad, PM*, I. 1. 16.

objects can be known by direct knowledge. If there is any object, whether it is far or near, then there must be its knowledge. For example, if a jar exists there must be its knower. As object, every object has its knower, so that such objects also must be known in omniscience. The possibility of *kevala* is also proved by the fact that there is no knowledge which could contradict it or which could show its impossibility[1]. If there were any knowledge which would contradict *kevala*, then Hemacandra asks, is that knowledge perception or inference ? Perception cannot do this, for as the *Mīmāṁsakas* recognise the senses apprehend only the objects which are present and with which they are related.

It may be supposed that perception contradicts *keuala*, not as knowing its object but as failing to know what is beyond it. If it is meant that perception has for its object determinate place and time and cannot know what is in another place and time, then we also agree. But if it is meant that perception cannot know all places and all times and so goes against *kevala*, then we would reply that there must be some kind of knowledge of all places and times and this is what is meant by the *kevala*. We can infer that there is the highest knowledge from the fact that knowledge has degrees. From this we can also infer that there is a person who knows all objects[2]. The mere fact that we do not come across such a person does not prove the absence of an omniscient being.

Inference also cannot contradict the possibility of *kevala*. For such an inference would require knowledge of the *pakṣa*, that is, the *kevala* itself. If *kevala* is known, its impossibility cannot be proved by an inference[3]. Hemacandra next considers an inference which has been used to prove that there is no omniscient person. The inference is of the following kind; "the person under consideration is not omniscient, for he is a person, as in the case of an ignorant person". This inference is not valid. What is meant by *vaktṛtva* which is the *hetu*? If it means the property of speaking what is known by a *pramāṇa*, then the *hetu* is *viruddha*, because such a *hetu* would rather prove

1. PM., I. 1. 17.
2. *prajñātiśayaviśrāntyādisiddhestatsiddhiḥ*, *ibid.*, I. 1. 16
3. *Ibid.*, I. 1. 17.

that the speaker is omniscient. If *vaktṛtva* means the property of speaking what is false, then there would be the fallacy of *siddhasādhana* or proving what is not disputed. If it means the property of merely being a speaker, then the *hetu* becomes *anaikāntika*, because we find that with the increase of knowledge one does not speak less; one finds on the other hand that one who knows more is also a better speaker. In the same way, the other *hetu*, that is, *puruṣatva* may also be refuted. If it means being a person unspoilt by defects, then the *hetu* is *viruddha* for it proves omniscience ; if it means being a person vitiated by defects, then the *hetu* becomes *siddhasādhana*. If it means merely being a person, then it may prove either omniscience or its absence and so becomes *anaikāntika*. Therefore, it does not show that the person is not omniscient[1].

The scriptures also cannot show the impossibility of omniscience. There is no scripture which is *apauruṣeya*; a scripture must have its origin in some omniscient person. Therefore, it cannot prove the absence of omniscience.

CONCLUSION

The *Āgamika* theory of perception of the Jainas is based on their conception of substance. According to the Jainas every substance (*dravya*) possesses some permanent qualities as well as some changing ones. The permanent qualities are the essential qualities of a substance; they are eternal and the changing qualities are the modes of the substance. The permanent qualities of the self are, for example, consciousness (*caitanya*) and the permanent qualities of the matter are *rūpa*, *rasa*, etc. Without consciousness there is no self and without *rūpa* etc. there is no matter. The changing qualities o fthe self are, for example, the different thoughts and ideas, and those of matter are blue, yellow, hardness softness etc. Thus every substance or *dravya* possesses two types of qualities. The permanent qualities of a *dravya* are called *guṇa* and the changing qualities are called *paryāya*. Therefore they define a substance or *dravya* as *guṇaparyāyavad dravyam*.

The Jainas hold that all the permanent and changing qualities cannot be apprehended by our sense-organs, nor are the

1. PM. I. 1. 17.

sense-organs able to apprehend an object in its true nature. It is the self only by which one can perceive an object in its true nature, or with all its (permanent and changing) qualities. Therefore, they define perception (in the *Āgamas*) as a knowledge derived from the self. They call it *pratyakṣa* or direct knowledge, as it arises in the self. They point out that, knowledge, caused by the sense-organs, is not direct; it is *parokṣa.* The knowledge according to the Jaina *Āgamas* which is based on the sense-organs cannot be called *pratyakṣa* or direct knowledge. Thus the *Āgamika* definition of the Jainas does not simply say that the direct sense object contact is *pratyakṣa* or perceptual knowledge. But they mean by *pratyakṣa* a direct knowledge arising in the self. When one apprehends an object by sense-organs, this apprehension would not be called direct experience of the object because it is based on the sense organs. It is indirect to the self. In this sense, the knowledge derived from the sense-organs is indirect to the self, therefore, the Jainas call sense perception indirect or *parokṣa* knowledge.

The Jaina view that the sense-organs are not able to apprehend the object with all its permanent and changing qualities, seems to be very reasonable because the sense-organs have limited capacities. In visual perception, for example, one sees the pot on the earth, he cannot see what is inside the pot, or the opposite side of the pot. Therefore, sense perception is not the highest type of knowledge, it is a limited process and therefore it cannot be called *pratyakṣa*. According to the Jainas *pratyakṣa* is that type of knowledge which is able to apprehend the object with all its permanent and changing qualities and that is possible only by the self. Therefore, *pratyakṣa* means the knowledge, arising in the self directly.

But in logical literature the Jainas accept sense perception as *pratyakṣa* or direct knowledge. Here the Āgamika *pratyakṣa* is called *mukhya pratyakṣa*; *mukhya* means 'superior'. Though they accept sense knowledge as *pratyakṣa* yet the superior is only that which arises in the self directly. And the knowledge of the object derived from the sense-organs is called *sāṁvyavahārika pratyakṣa*, the sensuous knowledge is *pratyakṣa* in *vyavahāra* or practice, or in the secondary sense ; the real *pratyakṣa* is the *mukhya pratyakṣa* which arises directly through the self.

The *sāṁvyavahārika pratyakṣa* or sense perception is not a superior kind of perception. It does not have the strength of the *mukhya pratyakṣa* nor does it arise in the self directly. But it is *pratyakṣa* in the sense that it is not based on any other knowledge. It manifests its object without the mediation of any other knowledge; therefore it is direct or clear (*viśada*). What is not direct in this sense, is not perception, just as inference.

Thus both kinds of *pratyakṣa* (*mukhya* and *sāṁvyavahārika*) are direct knowledge. The former is direct in one sense, and the latter is so in another sense.

The Jainas not only define *sāṁvyavahārika pratyakṣa* but also analyse the process involved in it. The process consists in the four stages of *avagraha*, *īhā*, *avāya* and *dhāraṇā*. The idea of four stages is original in this system. Though the other schools of Indian philosophy distinguish between *nirvikalpa* and *savikalpa* perception, yet this distinction is not as thorough as that of the Jainas. No other Indian system has given us such an account of the different stages of sense-perception.

The knowledge derived from the self directly is called *mukhya pratyakṣa* in logical literature. We may call it non-sensuous perception, because it is not caused by the sense-organs. There are three types of non-sensuous perception—the *avadhijñāna*, the *manaḥparyāyajñāna* and the *kevalajñāna*. The concept of non-sensuous knowledge in the Jaina philosophy is based on their metaphysics. According to the Jainas knowledge is the essential quality of the self. The pure self possesses infinite knowledge, but due to the veil of the *karmic* matters it cannot realise its true nature of infinite knowledge. When the obstruction of the *karmas* is destroyed, knowledge arises in the self. The self can then know objects directly without the help of the sense-organs, and this knowledge is higher than our ordinary sense knowledge, because there is no limitations of time and space in this knowledge. For these systems which do not regard knowledge as essential to the self—e.g., the *Nyāya*—there cannot be strictly speaking such a conception. The concept of *mukhya pratyakṣa* is thus based on their metaphysics, but it is also influenced by religious faith. Therefore, though the Jainas have tried to give inferences to prove the existence of such non-sensuous knowledge, yet it cannot be strictly proved logically as ordinary as every day experience of sense knowledge.

Regarding the nature of non-sensuous perception the Jainas are not very clear. They say simply that in *avadhijñāna* one apprehends material objects directly by the self; in *manaḥ-paryāyajñāna* the knowledge of other's mind is acquired; and in *kevalajñāna*, the self possesses the knowledge of all things, past, present and future and also of its own pure nature. The Jainas do not say much about the nature of non-sensuous perception. Does the self apprehend the objects in the same manner as our sense organs apprehend their objects? Or, do the objects come into contact with the self only in the shape of ideas? Or, is this knowledge a purely subjective experience like pleasure and pain? In some places we are told that the self sees all things in the same way as one sees the *āmalaka* fruit on his palm or just as one sees objects in the mirror. But these analogies are not enough to make us understand the real nature of non-sensuous perception.

Most systems of Indian philosophy believe in the possibility of an omniscient being. But the Jaina concept of omniscience has its own distinctive place amongst them. The Jainas hold that everybody can become an omniscient while most other systems believe only in God as the Omniscient being. According to the *Nyāya-vaiśeṣikas*, a *yogī* can acquire omniscience but this omniscience is not permanent; for, in the stage of release there would be no knowledge. Knowledge, according to them, is a non-eternal attitude of the self. Only God's omniscience is eternal but the omniscience acquired by the power of *yoga* cannot be eternal. But according to the Jainas, every self is omniscient ; due to the obstruction of the *karmic* matters, however, this omniscience is not manifested. By the practice of mental and bodily discipline and meditation everybody can destroy the *āvaraṇa* and can manifest the latent omniscience. As knowledge is the essential quality of self, the omniscience would be permanent, even in the stage of release.

Again, though the other systems (which believe in the possibility of an omniscient being), have given some arguments, yet these are not as strong as those given by the Jainas. A large part of the logical literature of the Jainas is full of the arguments for the possibility of omniscience.

Regarding the nature of omniscience or *kevalajñāna*, the Jainas are not very clear. They simply say that in *kevalajñāna* the self possesses knowledge of all objects, of past, present and future, so that nothing remains unknown to an omniscient person. But, as stated earlier, Kundakunda explains the nature of omniscience in a new way. He says that though a *kevalī* or the omniscient being perceives all objects of all time and of all place, yet it is so only from the *vyavahāra dṛṣṭi*. Really, however, a *kevalin* knows only himself or he has only an intuitive experience of the pure self. This explanation about the nature of *kevalajñāna* is very remarkable and true. In fact, when a self becomes pure, it becomes indifferent to all worldly things and shines in its own light, that is, the knowledge. Knowledge is the essential quality of the self, but due to the *āvaraṇa* of the *karmic* matter, it is not manifested. When the *āvaraṇa* is destroyed, there arises the knowledge. There is the knowledge of *self-realisation* or *ātmapratīti* or *ātmasākṣātkāra*. In this stage there is no difference between knowledge and self.

Thus, the explanation of *kevalajñāna* given by Kundakunda has its own important place in Jaina philosophy. This explanation is more satisfactory than that of the others. On this interpretation, the conception of omniscience or *kevalajñāna* gains a spiritual significance which it would lack if it were taken merely as a knowledge of all things.

APPENDIX

An Introduction to Jaina Logicians and their Logic

Jaina logic began from Siddhasena, who was the first great logician among the Jainas. But to some extent logical discussions are also to be found in the Āgamic literature like *Bhagavatī Sūtra*, *Sthānāṅga*, *Samavāyāṅga* and *Anuyoga* and some works on logic had been written between the Āgamic age and the time of Siddhasena. The chief logicians of this period were Ācārya Kundakunda and Umāsvāti.

Kundakunda

Kundakunda is supposed to belong to the first or second century A.D. He was the first amongst the Jainas to discuss the Āgamic themes in a logical manner. He not only expounded them on the basis of the *Āgamas* but also discussed the problems in the light of contemporary thought. Though Kundakunda did not discuss the problems of *pramāṇa*, yet his epistemology was influenced by the concept of *pramāṇa*. He explained *pratyakṣa* and *parokṣa* on the basis of the Āgamas. He pointed out that sense-knowledge could not be regarded as *pratyakṣa*; it was *parokṣa*. *Pratyakṣa* was that knowledge which arose in the self directly without the help of the sense-organs. He was also the first to discuss the problem of knowledge. He raised the question, whether knowledge is self-revealing or object-revealing (*svaprakāśa* or *paraprakāśa*) and established that knowledge is both self-revealing and object-revealing, just as a lamp revealed itself as well as the object. Later on, all the Jaina scholars accepted this view of knowledge. Kundakunda explained the *anekāntavāda* of the Āgamas in a systematic and clear way. Although he mentioned only the two *nayas* : *niścaya* and *Vyavahāra*, yet he tried to solve all difficult philosophical problems with the help of these two. The main works of Kundakunda are : *Pañcāstikāya*, *Pravacanasāra*, *Samayasāra*, *Niyamasāra*, *Aṣṭapāhuḍa*, *Daśabhakti*, *Sadāgamaṭīkā*, etc.

Umāsvāti

Umāsvāti was the first amongst the Jainas to use the Sanskrit language. Before him Jaina literature was written in Prakrit. *Tattvārtha ūtra* is Umāsvāti's main work. The subject-matter of *Tattvārtha Sūtra* is based on the *Āgamas* but it is written in a systematic way. There is considerable discussion about the nature, qualities and types of *dravya* (substance). Though there is not much discussion on *prameya*, *pramāṇa* and *naya*, yet Umāsvāti to some extent did define these concepts. The five types of knowledge of the Āgamas are according to him *pramāṇa*. He also classified *pramāṇa* into *pratyakṣa* and *parokṣa*. *Pratyakṣa* meant for him the immediate knowledge which arose in the self directly without the help of the sense-organs and *parokṣa* was defined as knowledge derived from the sense organs. He also described *naya* in a different way from that of the Āgamas. It may be said that though Jaina logic was not fully developed at the time of Kundakunda and Umāsvāti yet their writings exercised great influence on the development of Jaina logic.

Samantabhadra

After Kundakunda and Umāsvāti the period of Jaina logic began. As mentioned before, Siddhasena was the first great logician. We cannot also ignore the name of Samantabhadra in this connection (5th-6th century A.D.). Samantabhadra and Siddhasena may be called the founders of Jaina logic. Āptamīmāṁsā is the main work of Samantabhadra in which he introduced a new style to discuss the philosophical problems on the basis of *anekāntavāda*. He also gave a definition of *pramāṇa* in his Svayambhū Stotra, which may be viewed as the first logical type of definition of *Pramāṇa* amongst the Jainas. (*svaparāvabhāsakaṁ yathā pramāṇaṁ bhuvi buddhilakṣaṇam*).

Siddhasena

Siddhasena belonged to the seventh century A.D. The main works of Siddhasena are Sanmatitarka and Nyāyāvatāra. Sanmatitarka is written in Prakrit, in which he discussed the *nayas*, in a comprehensive manner on the view of *anekāntavāda*. Nyāyāvatāra has been called the foundation-stone of Jaina logic. In this work, he defined the *pramāṇa* not only on the basis of the Āgamic view but also according to his own independent thought and criticism of contemporary ideas on this matter. He classified *pratyakṣa* into two types : *anumāna* and *āgama*. This classification was influenced by the classification given by other schools of philosophy. Siddhasena was also the first Jaina logician who defined the four logical terms: *pramāṇa*, *pramātā*, *prameya* and *pramiti*.

Samanatbhadra and Siddhasena have done some preliminary work in the field of Jaina logic but in the meantime logic in other schools of philosophy had been developed more fully. There were great Buddhist logicians like Dignāga and Dharmakīrti. But amongst the Jainas there was no work comparable to Pramāṇa-samuccaya and Nyāyabindu.

Akalaṅka

Akalaṅka filled in this gap about the eighth century A.D. He was the first to expound the Āgamic theory of *pramāṇa* in a pure logical way. According to the Jaina Āgamas, *pramāṇa* is of two types : *pratyakṣa* and *parokṣa*. *Pratyakṣa* is the knowledge which arises immediately in the self without the help of sense-organs. *Akṣa* means the self, and knowledge derived from the self directly is called *Pratyakṣa*. *Parokṣa* is the knowledge which is not direct to the self but is derived with the help of sense-organs. *Pratyakṣa* is of three types, *avadhi*, *manaḥparyāya* and *kevala*. *Parokṣa* is of two types, *mati* and *śruta*. While all the systems of Indian philosophy accept as *pratyakṣa* all sensuous knowledge derived from the sense-organs, according to the Jaina Āgamas, sensuous knowledge is not *pratyakṣa*. Akalaṅka was faced with the problem, whether to accept the Āgamic view of *pratyakṣa*, or the contemporary theories of it. At first he defined *pratyakṣa* simply as clear knowledge (*viśadaṁ pratyakṣaṁ*), then he classified it into two types, the *sāṁvyavahārika pratyakṣa* and *mukhya pratyakṣa*. Knowledge derived from the sense organs was called *sāṁvyavahārika pratyakṣa* and knowledge which arises directly in the self was called *mukhya pratyakṣa*. Akalaṅka not only classified *pratyakṣa*, he also gave logical definitions of each kind of *pratyakṣa*. And on the basis of his definition of *pratyakṣa* he examined and criticised the definitions of *pratyakṣa* given by the other systems. Knowledge which was not *viśada* was *parokṣa* or indirect, according to him. He classified *parokṣa* into the following types : *smṛti*, *pratyabhijñā*, *tarka*, *anumāna* and *āgama*, all these being indirect knowledge.

Akalaṅka also explained the object (*viṣaya*) and the result (*phala*) of *pramāṇa* in a comprehensive and logical manner. He examined and discussed all logical problems and established some new facts in the field of logic. Laghīyasatraya, Nyāyaviniścaya, Pramāṇasaṅgraha and Siddhiviniścaya were his great works. He wrote commentaries on the Tattvārtha Sūtra of Umāsvāti and Āptamīmāmsā of Samantabhadra which are known as Tattvārthavārttika and Aṣṭaśatī respectively.

Vidyānanda

Vidyānanda was a great commentator on Akalaṅka. His commentary on Akalaṅka's Aṣṭaśatī, known as Aṣṭasāhasrī, is a valuable work in philosophy. Vidyānanda studied thoroughly all systems of philosophy. He was specially a great scholar of Mīmāṁsā school of Kumārila. He wrote Tattvārthaślokavārttika, (a commentary) on Umāsvāti's Tattvārtha Sūtra. In his own work Pramāṇaparīkṣā, he examined all the different views of *pramāṇa*. In Āptaprakāśa he rejected Kumārila's views and established the Jaina view regarding the possibility of omniscient being. Vidyānanda is supposed to belong to the 9th Century A. D.

Māṇikyanandi

Māṇikyanandi's Parīkṣāmukha was the first sūtra *grantha* in logic amongst the Jainas. It contained the following six chapters; *Pramāṇa pratyakṣa*, *parokṣa*, *viṣaya*, *phala* and *tadābhāsa*. In this the author discussed the logical problems in *sūtra* style. He examined other systems and by rejecting them established the Jaina views on logical grounds.

Prabhācandra

Prabhācandra was a follower of Māṇikyanandi. His commentary on Māṇikyanandi's Parīkṣāmukha is famous by the name of Prameya-kamalamārtaṇḍa. Nyāyakumudacandra is also a large commentary on Akalaṅka's Laghīyastraya. Prabhācandra was a great logician and acquired an important place in the whole of Indian logic and philosophy. In both the above commentaries he discussed the innumerable problems of logic and philosophy and by rejecting them he established the Jaina views. Prabhācandra belonged to the 13th century.

Abhayadeva Sūri

Abhayadeva Sūri was also a great commentator. He was the author of a commentary on Samantabhadra's Sanmatitarka in which he discussed the theories of different schools of philosophy.

Vādideva Sūri

Syādvādaratnākara is a large commentary on Pramāṇanayatattvālokālaṅkāra. Both these works were written by Vādideva Sūri. These were written in the style of Prameyakamalamārtaṇḍa and Nyāyakumudacandra, and the subject matter also was the same as that of those books. But there are also some discussions on *naya* and *vāda* which are not to be found in the Prameyakamalamārtaṇḍa and Nyāyakumudacandra. Vādideva Sūri also discussed and criticised the theories of the other systems. He belonged to the 12th century A.D.

Vādirāja

Vādirāja was also a great commentator. He wrote a big commentary on Akalaṅka's Nyāyaviniścaya by the name of Nyāyaviniścayavivaraṇa. There are three *prastāvas* in it, namely: *pratyakṣa*, *anumāna* and *pravacana*. He explained Akalaṅka's views very thoroughly.

Hemacandra

Pramāṇamīmāṁsā of Hemacandra (12th Century A.D.) has its own importance in Jaina logic. He also wrote on Prākṛta grammar and on various other subjects. Hemacandra was a great scholar of philosophy, logic, grammar and literature. His philosophy and logic were influenced by Akalaṅka. Though his work was based on the previous Jaina literature yet in many places he established his own views.

Yaśovijaya

Yaśovijaya of the 18th century was the last great Jaina logician. He studied *navyanyāya* and gave a new style to the Jaina logic. His main works are on *naya* and *anekāntavāda*. These are : *Nayapradīpa*, *Nayarahasya*, *Nayopadeśa*, Jainatarkabhāṣā and Jñānabindu.

Other Jaina logicians were Mallavādi, Sumati, Kumārasena, Kumāranandi, Anantavīrya I, Anantavīrya II and Anantakīrti. They have their own important place in the development of Jaina logic.

BIBLIOGRAPHY

I. SANSKRIT

Akalaṅkagranthatryayī : Akalaṅka, Singhi Jaina Series No. 12.

Aṣṭasāhasrī, (the *Ṭīkā* on Akalaṅka's *Aṣṭaśatī*) : Vidyānandi, Nirnaya Sagar Press, Bombay, 1915.

Jñānabinduprakaraṇa : Yaśovijaya, Singhi Jaina Series No. 13.

Karmagrantha I (Hindi Translation by Pt. Sukhalalji). Ātmānand Jaina Pustaka Pracāraka Maṇḍala, Agra, Series No. 27.

Karikāvalī—Muktāvalī : Viśvanātha, Chowkhamba Sanskrit Series, Banaras, 1951.

Niyamasāra : Kundakunda with the *Tātparyavṛtti*, Jaina Grantha Ratnakara, Bombay, 1916.

Nyāyāvatāravārttikavṛtti : Sidhasena, Singhi Jaina Series No. 20.

Nyāya Bhāṣya (*Vātsāyana Bhāṣya*) Chowkhamba Sanskrit Series, Banaras, 1924.

Nyāya Bindu : Dharmakīrti, Chowkhamba Sanskrit Series, Banaras, 1954.

Nyāyakumudacandra (the Commentary on Akalaṅka's *Laghīyastraya* : Prabhācandra, Manikya Chandra Digamber Jaina Granthamala, Bombay, 1938.

Nyāyamañjarī : Jayanta Bhaṭṭa, Chowkhamba Sanskrit Series, Banaras, 1956.

Nyāyaviniścayavivaraṇa (the Commentary on Akalaṅka's *Nyāyaviniścaya*) : Vādirāja, Bhāratīya Jñāna Pīṭha, Kāshī, 1949.

Pramāṇamīmāṁsā : Hemacandra, Singhi Jaina Series No. 7.

Pramāṇanayatatvāloka : Vādidevasūri, Shri Vijayadharma Suri Granthamala, Ujjain, Series No. 3.

Pramāṇanayatattvāloka (with Hindi Translation), Shri Jaina Gurukul Śikṣaṇa Saṅgha, Beyaver, 1942.

Prameyakamalamārtaṇḍa (the Commentary on Māṇikyanandi's *Parīkṣāmukha*) by Prabhācandra, Nirnaya Sagar Press, Bombay, 1941.

Sarvārtha Siddhi : Pūjyapāda (with Eng. Translation by S.A. Jaina) Vira Sasana Saṅgha, Calcutta, 1960.

Sāṁkhya Kārikā : Īsvarakṛṣṇa, with *Gauḍapāda-Bhāṣya*, Chowkhamba Sanskrit Series, Banaras, 1960.

Śāstradīpikā, Chowkhamba Sanskrit Series, Banaras.

Syādvāda Ratnākara I : Vādideva Sūri.

Tattvārtha Ślokavārttika : Vidyānandi (the Commentary on Umāsvāti's *Tattvārthasūtra*), Nirnaya Sagar Press, Bombay, 1918.

Tattvārthasūtra, vide *Tattvārthasūtra Bhāṣya* : Umāsvāti, Roy Chandra Jaina Śāstra Granthamala, Bombay), Series No. 14, 1932.

Tattvārthasūtra (with Hindi Translation by Pt. Sukhalalji), Shri Ātmānanda Janma Śatābdī Smāraka Granthamālā, Bombay, Series No. 1.

Tattvārthavārttika (*Rājavārttika*), the Commentary on *Tattvārthasūtra* : Akalaṅka, Bhāratīya Jñāna Pīṭha, Kāshī, 1953.

II. ENGLISH

BHATTACHARYA, H.S., *Reals in the Jaina Metaphysics*, The Seth Santi Das Khetry Charitable Trust, Bombay, 1965.

CHATTERJEE S.C., *Nyāya Theory of Knowledge*, University of Calcutta, 1965.

DASGUPTA S.N., *History of Indian Philosophy*, University Press, Cambridge, 1951.

KALGHATGI T.G., *Some Problems in Jaina Psychology*, Karnatak University, Dharwar, 1961.

MEHTA, M.L., *Jaina Psychology*, Sohanlal Jainadharma Pracharak Samiti, Amritsar, 1955.

SHAH, NAGIN J. *Akalaṅka's Criticism of Dharmakīrti's Philosophy*, L.D. Institute of Indology, Ahmedabad, 1967.

RADHAKRISHNAN, S., *Indian Philosophy*, 2 vols., George Allen & Unwin, London.

STCHERVATSKY, TH., *Buddhist Logic*, 2 vols., Dover Publications, Inc. New York.

SUKHALALJI, *Advanced Studies in Indian Logic and Metaphysics*, Indian Studies, Calcutta, 1961.

TATIYA, N.M., *Studies in Jaina Philosophy*, Jaina Cultural Research Society, Banaras.

III. HINDI

MALAVANIYA, D.S., *Agamayuga kā Jainadarśana*, Sanmati Jñāna Pīṭha, Agra, 1966.

SASTRI, PT. KAILASH CHANDRA, *Jaina Nyāya*, Bhāratīya Jñāna Pīṭha, Kāshi, 1966.

INDEX

—ooo—